24

JACKIE STEWART

PILOTE

JACKIE STEWART

TRIPLE-CROWNED KING OF SPEED

KARL LUDVIGSEN

Foreword by Chris Amon

Haynes Publishing

To Bernard Cahier

Friend, colleague and fine photographer whose many and valued contributions to motorsports over 50 years will only be appreciated when he writes a book of his own.

First published in 1998

British Library Cataloguing in Publication Data:
A catalogue record for this book is available from the British Library

ISBN 1 85960 436 6

Library of Congress catalog card no 98-72321

Haynes North America Inc.,
861 Lawrence Drive, Newbury Park, California 91320, USA.

Published by Haynes Publishing,
Sparkford, Nr Yeovil, Somerset BA22 7JJ, UK.

Tel: 01963 440635 Fax: 01963 440001
Int.tel: +44 1963 440635 Int fax: +44 1963 440001

E-mail: sales@haynes-manuals.co.uk
Web site: http://www.haynes.com

Designed and typeset by G&M, Raunds, Northamptonshire
Printed and bound in Great Britain by J. H. Haynes & Co., Ltd

Jacket illustrations

Front cover: With the intensity in the cockpit that was his trademark Jackie Stewart attacks the track in his Matra MS80 at Zandvoort in June 1969. The result: fastest lap, victory and a 12-point lead over Graham Hill on his way to his first World Championship. (Max Le Grand photo from the Ludvigsen Library)

Back cover: Zandvoort is also the setting for Stewart's strong drive to second place behind Jim Clark in the 1965 Dutch Grand Prix in his debut Formula 1 season. The well-made BRM 1½-litre V-8 suits his style down to the ground. (Max Le Grand photo from the Ludvigsen Library)

Frontispiece

Winning the French Grand Prix in 1969 at Clermont-Ferrand with a French Matra sponsored by France's state-owned oil company Elf is an achievement warranting a celebration by Jackie Stewart with a jeroboam of Moët & Chandon and his happy wife Helen. (Max Le Grand photo)

Contents

Introduction

Almost a quarter-century later, when preparing this book, I was surprised to realise that Jackie Stewart had needed me as much as I needed him. The newly-crowned Formula 1 World Champion Driver of 1969 needing my help? It seemed unlikely then and had done so for decades.

After his 1968 Vice-Championship John Young Stewart, in only his fifth full year in the Grand Prix circus, took the top prize by the widest margin and the highest points accumulation yet recorded. He stormed the season with his Matra chassis and Ford-Cosworth engine for the Tyrrell team. His was the brightest star in the firmament of motor racing.

With John Fitch, Jo Bonnier, Louis Stanley and others, Jackie agreed to join the organising board of directors of my brainchild, the Motor Racing Safety Society, created in 1969 to provide a forum for all professionals involved in reducing racing injuries and deaths. Stewart brought his newly-minted championship aura and his deep consideration of all aspects of racing to Geneva in March 1970 for an all-day meeting of the Society.

"Stewart was sensational," I wrote in my notes on the meeting at the Hotel Intercontinental. "He was with us all day and he was most helpful throughout." Jackie commented on the physical effects of the Cosworth V-8's vibration, on the acceleration (g.) forces affecting the Formula 1 driver (up to 1.3 g. in braking then, tests in South Africa showed) and on trends in seating positions and head and neck angles. His interest, his knowledge and his credibility were a boon to our budding venture. "He has a new fan in me," I concluded my notes.

So delighted was I by the World Champion's active participation that I failed to see the situation from Jackie's own perspective until I looked back from the vantage point of the late 1990s. He needed us too!

Our society was another voice raised in favour of greater safety in motor racing. By supporting us, Stewart was shrewdly encouraging an ally in a campaign in which he had been thought by many to be more active than was appropriate for a Great Racing Driver. In those controversial days Jackie needed all the allies he could enlist.

This book about the amazing career of J. Y. Stewart

OBE (in 1972) launches head-first into the issue of his drive for safer racing, and not just because I was one of his associates in that campaign. It does so because we need the perspective of the end of the 1990s to understand those struggles of a third of a century ago. This is the first biography that assesses Jackie Stewart's life and work from that vantage point. Indeed, it is the first book-length biography of Stewart.

I took full advantage of the books, periodicals and press cuttings on file at the Ludvigsen Library. Years ago I had planned to write about Jackie; the research materials were still to hand. Fortunately for his biographer Stewart has never been slow to put his views forward in print. The gift of the gab noted by so many of his colleagues has been a gift to this writer also.

Special thanks are owed to the publishers of several works for their permission to print quotations from Chairman Jackie. At the height of his racing career Stewart spoke at length to American author Peter Manso about his life and work. Eric Dymock, who shared some of Jackie's first motorsporting experiences, wrote about the driver in articles and in a book about his first World Championship season.

Other authors and journalists whose writings about Jackie Stewart have been of value are Barrie Gill, Elizabeth Hayward, Mary Schnall Heglar, Chris McCall, Nigel Roebuck, David Tremayne and Eoin Young. Among the racing drivers who gave their perspectives of Jackie over the years are Jack Brabham, Emerson Fittipaldi, Graham Hill and Jody Scheckter. Tony Rudd's comments on his star signing to the BRM strength have been of great interest, as have the views of Ken Tyrrell. Jim Hall discussed with me the dramatic debut of the Chaparral 2J at Watkins Glen in Stewart's hands and Donald Davidson helped with details of Jackie's Indy 500 exploits.

I was encouraged to show and tell the Stewart story by the Library's holdings of Max Le Grand's photography, which depict Jackie's career from his spectacular explosion onto the world of Formula 3 racing in 1964. Max approached his photography with the eye of an artist; I have aimed to give it the scope it deserves. Other Library holdings that contributed to this book are the work of Stanley Rosenthall, Ted Eves, Ove Nielsen and the author.

I couldn't have done justice to the Stewart saga without the personal photography of his friend and fellow Scot, Graham Gauld. Graham also described the early Stewart years in his engrossing and personal book, *Ecurie Ecosse*. Other fine photographers who rallied to the cause are Jesse Alexander, Bernard Cahier and Michael Cooper. I hope they will be happy with the way their work has been used to display, first of all, fine photography, with the concomitant aim of depicting highlights of the career of a great racing champion.

When thoughts turned to an appropriate person to write a foreword, friend and former colleague Chris Amon was my first choice. I worked with Chris on several projects, one of which was sponsorship in the Can-Am series for his Ferrari 612 in 1969 and March 707 in 1970. As drivers Chris and Jackie were closely matched; they formed a perfect team to drive a sports-racing Ferrari at Brand Hatch in 1967 and some of their Grand Prix clashes were the stuff of legend. Many thanks indeed, Chris, for the foreword.

At the Ludvigsen Library Paul Parker helped greatly with photo research and attribution and the annotation of the bibliography. Darryl Reach and his team at Haynes Publishing have been hugely competent and supportive. Many thanks also to my assistant Inga Pone, and to my wife Annette and her son Sam Turner, for their encouragement of this project. As always, any errors of omission or commission are mine alone.

Now, tighten the harness that straps a sizzling Cosworth V-8 to your backside, grip that thick-rimmed wheel, depress the clutch, tweak the tiny gearstick to clatter the Hewland box into first, massage that throttle pedal and get ready for a fast ride over the world's great race tracks with a master of his sport: triple World Champion John Young Stewart.

Karl Ludvigsen
Islington, London
April 1998

Foreword

by Chris Amon

In this book Karl Ludvigsen brings out very well the huge impact that Jackie Stewart made on the racing scene, an impact that few before or since have even vaguely approached. Many of us, both at the time of his racing career and since, can be eternally grateful for his achievements.

The determination, tenacity and sheer time that he, along with Jo Bonnier, devoted to the safety issue – often in the face of very adverse criticism – was amazing. I was quoted at the time as being critical of Armco barriers, and I was. I didn't like them. But I was certainly one hundred percent behind the principles of safety that Jackie and Jo were trying to put into place.

So much of what exists today has stemmed from their efforts. Had they not been initiated I believe that Grand Prix racing would not have survived. In hindsight I believe that we were treading a very fine line between the acceptance, or not, by modern society of the mortality rates which we were experiencing.

Another area of the sport on which Jackie had a lasting impact was the professional side. Whilst Stirling Moss may have been the first truly professional driver, during his career Jackie upped the ante considerably. This was once again in the face of much criticism, usually from those not receiving the financial gains.

Many of the drivers of today who are receiving what in our terms could be considered kings' ransoms can be grateful for the efforts of Jackie. These have not only been of benefit to the top drivers but have flowed on to many involved in the sport and at all levels.

Once again this was something that Jackie had carefully thought through. I remember playing golf with him at Watkins Glen – he was playing, I was hacking around – and the subject of money came up. I said to him, "Jackie, don't you think there is a chance you'll kill the golden goose?" His reply was, "Chris, no one has, nor will they ever, pay me more than they think I am worth." I had no answer.

One aspect of Jackie's career that Karl covers in the book is how near he came to driving for Ferrari in 1968. I am happy to say that I was probably the principal instigator of this approach to Jackie. While I was well aware that his arrival at Ferrari would have greatly increased the inter-team rivalry, I believe his presence within Ferrari would have had nothing but positive results.

I am sure that his personal determination would have led to messages getting through much better to the people concerned, such as concern about the lack of truly competitive engines. I also believe that he would have been much more successful than either Jacky Ickx or myself at diverting the wrath of the Italian media away from Ferrari's drivers and towards the cars.

I suppose, on a purely selfish note, that the chance to compete against Jackie in identical Ferraris was very appealing. We both drove March-Fords in 1970 but in that case many of the key components such as the teams, tyres, dampers and at times the engines were quite different, which led to one or the other having a significant advantage on occasion.

I am often asked to rank the great drivers of all time. Whilst that may seem a very complicated and difficult question, I believe that the answer is very simple: a driver who was exceptional in a specific era would have been exceptional in any era and Jackie is certainly one of those.

That answer often leads to the next question: How do you rate Jackie Stewart with Jim Clark? My answer is that in terms of sheer pace I think there was probably little difference between them. Perhaps Jackie had to work a little harder than Jimmy to achieve it.

In my opinion, Jackie was not only one of the greatest drivers of all time, he was also probably the most complete. By that I mean that his whole approach to racing, both in and out of the cockpit, was organised, thought out and planned to the last detail.

Jackie gave the strong impression that he would succeed at any endeavour he undertook. His capacity for work was phenomenal. His schedule, which accounted for almost every minute of the day, was such that it made me tired even thinking about it.

In this book I believe Karl has brought out very well one of the qualities that I think stands Jackie aside from many of the greats: despite all his achievements and his huge determination and will to succeed, he always maintained his approachability and his sense of humour. He was devoid of the inner complexities and hang-ups that have characterised some others.

Karl's book on the life, so far, of this truly exceptional man has revived many memories for me. It has been a great honour and privilege to be asked to write a Foreword to a book on Jackie Stewart.

GOODYEAR
elf

CHAPTER 1

Mister 101 Percent

En route to his third World Championship in 1973 Jackie Stewart saw, with some satisfaction, real progress in his campaign to make racing safer. "A lot of people criticised me personally," he recalled, "saying I was trying to wrap everyone in cotton wool. Dreamers, all of them. Christ Almighty, when did *they* ever hit an Armco barrier at 150 miles per hour? They talked about barriers as if they were candyfloss! Motor racing will never be safe. There will always be accidents and there will always be fatalities. But at least people now accept there's no room for *unnecessary* hazards. People with half a brain, anyway ...

"I obviously didn't go on this so-called safety crusade for personal benefit," Jackie told Eoin Young. "That's fairly obvious from the number of attacks I've had. I look back almost with amusement when I read some of the attacks that people burdened on me and then I read what they write today. It's a totally different pattern, and this change in attitude pleases me to some extent. The fact that so many more people have become aware of the hazards is satisfying and I hope I've done something towards that."

He certainly did. Jackie Stewart sees both challenges and opportunities, and boxes his internal compass to set a resolute course toward their mastery. Rightly enough, we are aware years later, Stewart discerned no conflict between his commitment to world-class race driving, on the one hand, and his campaign to reduce injuries to drivers and spectators alike on the other hand. That the two were related was coincidental. That so few people could comprehend this at the time was deplorable.

Racing fans and the press who follow the sport have trouble assessing a man like Stewart who has room in his capacious cranium for more than one idea at a time. They think a great motor racer must be consumed by the sport, must live and breathe it night and day to the exclusion of all else. Drivers like Mario

The relentless attacking style of Jackie Stewart in a Tyrrell-Ford dominates his 1971 and 1973 Championship seasons. In the 1971 British GP (front row of the grid, fastest lap, victory) Bernard Cahier captures the image that no driver welcomes in his mirrors.

Andretti, Gerhard Berger, Gilles Villeneuve, Nelson Piquet, Denny Hulme and Emerson Fittipaldi who were racers first, foremost and always deserve the admiration of their many fans.

The sport's followers break out all nervy when a driver seems to be capable of more than fast motoring. Consider Roger Penske, Niki Lauda, Keke Rosberg, Jody Scheckter and, dare I mention him, Nigel Mansell – great racers all who were also able to compete effectively in arenas that didn't demand their donning triple layers of Nomex. Somehow they're suspect, these men who can excel in the business world or in other sports or both. The same suspicion coloured perceptions of Stewart's career.

It's easy enough to grasp the reason why. We have to blame the green-eyed monster. Followers of the sport envy men who have the skill to win races and championships and at the same time – damn their hide! – are savvy enough to master quite different challenges. Those of us who will never race a Formula 1 car think that someone who can should be satisfied with that as the pinnacle of his life's achievement!

Some people are not so satisfied, and J. Y. Stewart OBE is among them. This was the key to his ability to compartmentalise his life while he was an active driver: here racing so relentlessly that he demoralised the opposition, there organising a boycott of a race if that one tree on the outside of a corner stayed in place. Whatever Jackie does he attacks with the determination of a true Scot. Where others saw a conflict between these parallel objectives he saw only two separate, albeit related, tasks that were both worth performing.

Jackie first spotted the possibilities of greater safety in racing when he competed in the United States. In 1965 he raced in the final West Coast sports-racing events and tested at Indianapolis, where he led the 500-mile race in 1966 until an engine failure close to the finish. "I went to America and found out over there that they were doing quite a few other things, looking at new materials that were of benefit to us," he told Peter Manso. "So in a sense my concern for safety started early and has developed. Motor racing will always be a dangerous sport because one is always going much too fast for the things around you. But being professionals and racing as often as we do, we have to try and look out for ourselves in the best manner we can."

Often enough Stewart has referenced a severe smash in his two-litre BRM during a rainstorm at the 1966 Belgian Grand Prix as the catalyst for his interest in racing safety. "I went off the road at Spa, Francorchamps, at some 150-odd miles per hour, aquaplaned, completely through no fault of my own. Seven drivers from the best in the world crashed on the first corner. I wasn't one of them. I crashed on the second corner! I went off the road and knocked down a couple of walls and part of a house and a few other things and luckily got off with very light injuries. The electric pumps were going, the power was still on, so the fire risk was enormous. Now this is not a pleasant experience.

"I had broken my collar bone and dislocated a shoulder and I had some ribs cracked," he said to Manso. "I had a bit of a sore back and a little bit of concussion. When I was lying in the hospital I can remember thinking that perhaps I might be better doing something else. But it never gave me any serious thought of retiring from racing."

Jackie's friends, however, remember a crash two years earlier at Oulton Park that nearly truncated a budding driving career. His Ecurie Ecosse Cooper Monaco's tyres were cold when Stewart set out on a practice lap. "Jackie flew off the road and hit a tree at such an angle that the car literally placed itself vertically up the trunk," wrote Graham Gauld, who was later told by the driver following Stewart that "to this day I don't think Jackie realises how lucky he was because when he hit the tree there was a branch sticking out and I swear it missed his head by about six inches. Six inches another way and ..."

"I climbed down a branch of the tree to get out of the car," Stewart recalled, "and it was a sorry sight." At Spa in 1966 he had to endure a much longer wait while team-mate Graham Hill, who had also crashed in the wet, went to find a wrench to release the steering wheel that was binding him into the wreck, deeply crushed on its right flank. Jackie's spirits lifted when he heard the blades of a helicopter overhead: "I thought the chopper had come for me but, in fact, it was doing some filming for the movie *Grand Prix*. And this was a bit of a disappointment."

There were more disappointments to come. Stewart: "There were no doctors and there was nowhere to put me. They in fact put me in the back of a van. Eventually an ambulance took me to a first aid spot near the control tower and I was left on a stretcher, on the floor, surrounded by cigarette ends. I was put into an ambulance with a police escort and the police escort lost the ambulance, and the ambulance didn't know how to get to Liège. I realised that if this was the best we had there was something sadly wrong: things wrong with the race track, the cars, the medical side, the fire-fighting and the emergency crews. It was ridiculous."

Stewart might have excused some of these Keystone Kops antics at Oulton Park or Charterhall. But this was the Belgian Grand Prix, one of the star events of the world's premier car-racing championship. He had arrived at the top of his sport only to discover that Formula 1 racing had no safety infrastructure worthy of the name, either to minimise injury to its participants or to tend to their injuries after a crash. It was a sobering realisation and an epiphany for the 27-year-old racing driver. Fortunately for the sport, Stewart decided to take an interest in racing safety.

Jackie's first action was to ensure that subsequent BRM race cars had suitable spanners taped to the steering wheel. His American racing experience led to the fitting of safety harness to his Formula 1 BRM in 1967 and he was soon experimenting with improved helmets and new materials for racing suits. He arranged for a personal physician to be on hand at his races and took medical advice on the best race-day diet.

But Stewart's activism was not for his own benefit alone. He understood the sport well enough to know that it could not afford another tragedy on the scale of Le Mans in 1955, where a Mercedes-Benz 300SLR killed 81 spectators and its driver. That resulted in cancelled events, the barring of racing in Switzerland and the resignation of the American sanctioning body. A repetition could eradicate motorsports altogether.

"Our first concern is to eliminate all possibility of cars reaching spectator areas," Stewart said in 1969 on behalf of the Grand Prix Drivers' Association and colleagues Jo Bonnier and Jochen Rindt. Cue the entry of the much-discussed Armco barriers, named after the American steel company that makes them. Stewart: "The drivers know better than anyone what a projectile, which a racing car really is, can do if it goes haywire." The aim of the course-flanking barriers was to keep the cars away from the spectators.

For the sinuous road course at Barcelona's Montjuich Park the Spanish spent some £25,000 on Armco for their 1969 race. "They took our word that the whole track needed barriers," Stewart recalled, "and let there be no mistake, they prevented what would certainly have been a tragedy of 1955 Le Mans proportions. There is no doubt in my mind that the Spanish organisers saved the lives of Graham Hill and Jochen Rindt. Not only that, they saved the lives of many spectators" when the Lotuses of both drivers crashed after the failure of the mountings of their high-flying wings.

The Austrian Rindt, who lived like Jackie near Geneva, was one of his best off-track friends and the on-track rival he most respected. Their families and children were close. That Jochen Rindt died after the nose of his Lotus slammed under the Armco during practice at Monza in 1970 was, in Stewart's view, due as much to disabling off-track politics as to his injuries.

"His jugular was cut," Jackie remembered, "and there must have been massive haemorrhaging, but this probably didn't have to be fatal. Even if Jochen was dead when they took him out of his car, if his heart had stopped beating, had they got him to the

Medical Unit quickly it is possible that with a good anaesthetist he could have been brought back to life."

Only 20 yards from the ambulance where poor Rindt was being treated in primitive conditions sat the Grand Prix Medical Unit, a mobile field hospital which regrettably was not welcomed by all the circuit administrations – especially those at Monza. This, said Stewart, had been equipped through the efforts of BRM team chief Louis Stanley "with the latest mechanical devices for resuscitation and all the blood he might have needed, and an air-conditioned, fully germ-free operating theatre offering him every possible chance of survival. And it was not used. Why? There is no explanation but politics. This is something that we have to obliterate from motor racing."

Followers of modern motorsports will look back on these tales from an earlier era with bafflement. They sit a long way from the track so there's room for run-off areas and gravel traps. Protective cockpit structures and strong monocoques with programmed-crush sides are taken for granted. Fire extinguishing crews are on the spot, as are Formula 1's medical supremo Professor Sid Watkins and his team, to deal with emergencies.

From time to time we must be reminded to sharpen up our act, as by the deaths of Ayrton Senna and Roland Ratzenberger at Imola in 1994 and the grievous injuries to Karl Wendlinger in the following race at Monaco. But we now accept that a racing driver who has been let down by his car, by the track, by a competitor or by his own actions need not be maimed or killed as a penalty. BRM's Tony Rudd put it well: "Racing drivers of Jackie's calibre or even of a lesser standard are in very short supply, and the waste of human life when it could so easily be avoided was indefensible. There is a fine difference between dangerous and wasteful."

Jackie Stewart put his prestige and reputation on the line to achieve awareness of this, both in his own era and for subsequent generations of drivers. "It might disappoint those who claim that Nuvolari or Caracciola or Fangio never complained about safety precautions," he said in the 1970s, "to know that Fangio thinks that Spa's too dangerous to race on today. Fangio is sensible enough to realise that things are changing all the time. Journalists are not using the same cameras they used ten years ago and we are not using the same cars. Things change and the modern way to go about motor racing or anything else is to introduce as much safety into it as you possibly can. Those who criticise may well continue to do so, but more and more they will appear to be merely eccentrics."

Speaking on behalf of the Grand Prix Drivers' Association, Swedish publishing heir Jo Bonnier was in the vanguard of those who pressed for safer racing, especially after the shocking death in 1968 of Jim Clark – ace of aces who, like Senna, was thought blessed with immortality behind the wheel. Jackie was told of the death of friend and mentor Clark – "a terrible shock" – when he was walking the track at Jarama in Spain for a GPDA inspection. That bitter season also claimed leading drivers Mike Spence, Ludovico 'Lulu' Scarfiotti and Jo Schlesser. "If you raced for five years," Stewart calculated, "there was a two out of three chance that you would die."

In 1969 Stewart could add the prestige of a World Championship to the safety campaign. None could accuse the Scotsman of being a talker, not a doer. Stewart knew this. "I think it's totally wrong," he said, "that a young apprentice racing driver coming along at an antiquated race track, with facilities that are historic, dies and finishes his career because we are not responsible enough to push for this sort of movement. I think it's in my hands as a racing driver at this time – a racing driver who people are willing to listen to – to promote this sort of action." Stewart did command attention. And he wasn't reluctant to exploit his stardom to benefit the sport.

"There are those who have said I remove the romance from the game, that with me as Champion it was no longer the swashbuckling spectacular it had been," Stewart mused. "When I campaigned for more realistic safety measures, these people said I had no guts. Well, I have the track record to answer that."

I'll say he does. Stewart never sacrificed speed for safety. Tony Rudd, whose BRMs Jackie drove from 1965 through 1967, said that "Jackie would give every race his maximum effort. I never minded Jackie's search for increased safety because once the flag fell he gave you 101 percent."

At Watkins Glen in 1970 Jackie drove a Chaparral for Texan Jim Hall, who wondered what he'd let himself in for. "When he got there all he could talk about was safety. He looked at the track, at the guard rails and at the car and he asked for changes in the seat belts and so forth, and they were made. But he had it on his mind so much that I thought, 'This could be a problem, it could affect his driving.' But as soon as he got behind the wheel he shut that off completely and he went for it. He gets in the car, he pulls down his visor and he *stands* on it! I was impressed by him. He did everything that he was supposed to do for us – and then some."

Jody Scheckter, Jackie's successor in Team Tyrrell, had a chance to observe the man at close quarters. "Jackie was without question the best of his era," said the talented South African. "As well as being a 'natural' driver, he was always coming up with ideas on how to improve the way he drove a particular track. He never stopped thinking about ways of doing things better than other drivers, ways that would mean that *he* was always the man to beat. When he retired as World Champion at the end of the 1973 season, he had been the man to beat in Grand Prix racing for five or six years."

When the two drivers were still battling against each other on the tracks Emerson Fittipaldi told Elizabeth Hayward: "There is no doubt in my mind that at the moment Jackie Stewart is the best driver in the world. I think Jackie is the most complete driver. He is a very technical driver, and I think his biggest advantage is that he can go round a circuit with a new car and can find what is wrong with it; he knows what has to be changed and he can give exactly the right information to the mechanics. He can always pick out a fault as though he has little wires attached to him from all over the car. So he can always use his car on the limit."

In fact, as Stewart was the first to admit, he did *not* rely on his youthful understanding of car technology to give specific instructions to his pit team. "I don't profess to be a designer of racing cars," he said to Peter Manso, "so therefore I have a designer who works on it. I try to relate what the car is doing to him the best way that I can. I try to paint a picture to him as clear and as colourful as I can so that he can read back and see that picture as well as he can see a photograph. Now if I colour it correctly, the chances are that he's going to bring out on paper and in mathematics the faults that I feel through my backside."

Nevertheless if Fittipaldi thought that Stewart had the capability that he attributed to him, it gave the Scot an advantage over the Brazilian. The same applied to another comment of Emerson's to Hayward: "He is a driver that you rarely see make a mistake, spinning off or doing anything wrong. It is difficult for him to make a mistake." In fact, as these pages will disclose, Jackie made his full share of mistakes behind the wheel but he had a knack for making them in practice or where they weren't in plain view.

Stewart himself pointed this out to Jody Scheckter, who had triggered a mêlée at Silverstone by spinning in the midst of the field on the first corner of the first lap: "He made me feel a whole lot better by pointing out that he'd made almost exactly the same mistake as I had and for exactly the same reason – trying too hard. He was just lucky that he'd done it way over on the far side of the circuit where there was hardly anybody to see it and not in front of the pits and grandstand."

The annual *Autocourse* reflected the general view in its summary of the 1973 Formula 1 season: "Whatever other thoughts he may have had before a race, whatever his opinion of a track or its safety arrangements, Stewart got into the cockpit of his sleek Tyrrell-Ford and tried his very hardest. The ultra-professional. In years to come his name will be compared with Nuvolari, Fangio, Ascari and Clark in the inevitable arguments about 'who was the greatest?'"

Autocourse is respected for its annual rankings of each season's top Grand Prix drivers. This is potent fuel for a winter's bench-racing. From 1968 to 1973, six full seasons, Jackie Stewart sat at the top of the *Autocourse* honour roll, even in 1970 when his friend Rindt was the posthumous World Champion and Jackie, hit by a rash of Ford engine failures, was 'only' equal fifth with Brabham in the World Championship. Tedious though Jackie's safety lectures were to some journalists, they respected his prowess on the track.

In 1965, his first full season in Formula 1, Stewart was third in the Championship rankings. This, wryly admitted his BRM team-mate Graham Hill, "was a pretty good debut." BRM was eclipsed the next two seasons, and with them Jackie's points tally, but he had the pleasure and frustration of leading but not winning at Indianapolis in 1966. Stewart bounced back with second in the 1968 Formula 1 standings driving a Matra-Ford. The same combination brought him his first World Championship in 1969.

Ken Tyrrell and Ford shared the huge risk of building a Ford-powered car of his own for Jackie. It took the Scot to his second Championship in 1971. In a difficult 1972 season Jackie was Vice-Champion behind new rival Emerson Fittipaldi. The order was reversed in 1973 when Stewart won his third World Championship with a record-high points total. In contesting 99 World Championship races he won 27, just pipping Jim Clark's 25. He had been on pole 17 times and set 15 fastest race laps. He also won five of the 21 non-Championship Formula 1 races he entered.

This was a record of unprecedented excellence. Jackie Stewart was the first racing driver since Juan Manuel Fangio to win more than two World Championships, and his successes came against formidable opposition. The British Racing Drivers' Club celebrated his skills with a sprinkling of six BRDC Gold Stars through the years 1968 to 1973.

When *F1 Racing* magazine ranked the greatest British Grand Prix drivers it placed only Moss and Clark ahead of Stewart and called the latter "the first modern Grand Prix driver." Not a bad result, in retrospect, for a man whose goal had been to be a good club racer who could cross the border from time to time to show those Englishmen that Scots were not all slow coaches – and relieve them of some of their precious pounds sterling.

Opposite: If you had been trapped in a BRM looking as shopworn as this one after a crash on a wet Spa circuit on 13 June 1966 you, like Jackie, would want to be sure that your future racers carried a spanner that would help remove the steering wheel. His interest in improved safety enrols Stewart as a tester of new fire-resistant suit materials; some offer so little ventilation that they parboil the driver.

Overleaf: Author Karl Ludvigsen captures the long shadow that Jackie Stewart casts over his Formula 1 rivals in the pit lane at Watkins Glen in 1971. Jackie wins six Championship races that season on his way to his second driver's crown.

Second overleaf: The teamwork of Stewart, Tyrrell, Matra, Ford-Cosworth, Dunlop and Elf finds devastating form in 1969, Jackie's first Championship year. Michael Cooper pictures Stewart scoring his second win of the season at Barcelona's Montjuich Park circuit in the last Formula 1 race before high wings are banned.

JACKIE STEWART
BLOOD GROUP
O RH +

GOODYEAR
elf

DUNLOP
elf
7
Autolite

DUNL
ECURIE
ECOSSE

CHAPTER 2

Ecurie Ecosse to Can-Am

"After I drove the Tojeiro for the first time David asked me where I wanted to have the foot-rest fitted. The mechanics had one made out of alloy and riveted it into the car in the paddock. This was really something. I had never experienced anything like it before and it was a great moment of pleasure and excitement. I remember thinking this was the big-time, the end of the rainbow and at that time it is as far as I imagined I would go in motor racing." Thus did Jackie Stewart recall his introduction to Scotland's leading racing team, Ecurie Ecosse, and its patron David Murray.

Stewart was sleepless for three straight nights before that drive at Scotland's Charterhall circuit in 1963 in the mid-engined coupé built for Murray's Edinburgh-based team by John Tojeiro with its tuned Buick V-8 engine. This was his first-ever drive in a full-blooded sports-racing car and it was, and remains, a memorable occasion. "I won the race, too," Jackie added.

Jackie Stewart's laid-back style in the Ecurie Ecosse Cooper Monaco brings him eight race victories in a difficult car before he crashes it so comprehensively at Oulton Park in 1964 that it is remade as a single-seater. Here he is winning at Charterhall in Scotland in September 1963.

Those sleepless nights reflected the ambivalence towards motor racing of the 24-year-old Scot, to whom "David Murray was a god." He hugely enjoyed fast driving and had found that he was quick enough to win club races. This was an enjoyable hobby but surely no way to make a proper living. "I was always terribly ambitious to make money," Jackie told Peter Manso. "I can remember when I was very young – before I started working in the family garage – looking at people who had Mark V Jaguars or a Bentley or a Lagonda and thinking, 'My God, they're rich, how am I ever going to have things like that?'"

Young Jackie had ample exposure to wealthy people and their fine motorcars in the circles in which his family moved in Scotland – not because the Stewarts were rich themselves but because they served the needs of the rich. Grandfather Stewart was a game-keeper on the estate of industrialist Lord Weir at

Eaglesham, near Renfrew, north-west of the centre of Glasgow on the south bank of the River Clyde.

Lord Weir took a special interest in Bob Stewart, the gamekeeper's son, who in the 1920s had shown an aptitude for motorcycle racing. When the latter was ready to make his way in the world the peer helped him buy what was then a small garage in the hamlet of Milton where the Glasgow road approached Dumbarton on the north of the Clyde. Dumbarton is an industrial town whose main claim to fame is the distilling of Ballantine's scotch whisky.

The Dumbuck Garage and the bungalow next to it became the epicentre of the lives of Bob Stewart, his wife Jean and their two sons who had arrived relatively late on the scene – Jimmy and his younger brother Jackie, who was born on 11 June 1939 at Milton. In British parlance, of course, a 'garage' sells petrol, services cars and often also sells them, in this case with the distinction of Austin and Jaguar agencies. Dumbuck earned laurels as well with its servicing skills and the speed tuning of its customers' cars, although thrifty Scots considered its services rather pricey.

Both boys saw the garage as their future. While Jimmy looked after sales, Jackie was trained in service. His education at Dumbarton Academy ended when he was 15. Looking back, Jackie says he was "stupid, dumb and thick" in his schooldays, when he was taunted for his ineptitude. Only when he was 45 did he discover that he had been dyslexic all along. He compensated with his competitiveness in school sports, playing football for the school and then the county.

Leaving school, young Stewart was enrolled in a City and Guilds Apprenticeship as a motor mechanic. Studying at night and working at the garage by day he started on the petrol pumps, progressed to the grease racks and then to the workshop. By his early 20s Jackie was running the tuning side of the garage and looking after high-performance cars.

Of the latter there was no shortage because Jimmy Stewart had taken up race driving in 1953, when Jackie was 14. Jimmy started with the inevitable MG TC and then one of the more ambitious cars of the day, the Healey Silverstone. To qualify Jimmy to race for David Murray's Ecurie Ecosse his father bought him a brand-new C Type Jaguar, which he drove with considerable panache. His impressionable younger brother attended the races and pestered the drivers to autograph the pages of a scruffy brown book he still treasures.

But at 14 Jackie had been bitten by a powerful new obsession of his own, and it had nothing to do with cars. "God gave me a pair of hands to drive a car," he said, "and pull a trigger." Pulling triggers came naturally to a lad whose grandfather was a gamekeeper and whose father was meticulous about the etiquette of shooting. "It was always an ambition to get a gun in my hand," Jackie told Elizabeth Hayward. "I was trained the right way, starting with shooting rabbits up behind our house."

After Lord Weir's grouse shooting party had sharpened their aim with a spot of trapshooting on the estate, young Stewart would borrow the trap and send up a few clays of his own. He soon found it harder to miss the spinning 'pigeons' than hit them. Jackie claims he won the first trapshooting competition he entered at 14 because it was on New Year's Day and his rivals were still blind drunk.

In 1955, the year his brother retired from racing Stewart, then 16, was on the Scottish trapshooting team and in 1956, at Bournemouth, he won the West of England Championship. His eye was in and he kept on winning: Scottish, Welsh, English, Irish and British Championships and the European and Mediterranean Coupe des Nations. Jackie seemed a certainty for the two-man team that would represent Britain at the 1960 Rome Olympics.

The selection shoot-off among three contenders was a formality, with Stewart in the lead as usual. But then – disaster. "I suddenly lost eight targets out of 25, something I'd never done before, and I was relegated to Reserve," he told Hayward. "I did not travel to Rome. It still rankles, because it was something I had a terrible ambition to do. I wanted *desperately* to be a member of the Olympic team. To be in the Olympics was something bigger than being a Formula 1 driver – it was *big*. Oh, it was very annoying."

Jackie would shoot competitively for two more seasons. But in that fateful year of his majority, 1960, he also had a first real taste of another sport: motor racing. He had been befriended by a man he admired, motorcycle racer Bob McIntyre. In 1957 the first man to lap the awesome Isle of Man TT course at better than 100 miles per hour, McIntyre was considering a conversion from his Gileras to four-wheeled racers and borrowed an AC Bristol from a Dumbuck Garage customer to drive down to the challenging, hilly Oulton Park circuit near Chester to try his skills. Appropriately, he asked Jackie Stewart to ride shotgun.

"We both thrashed round there for a morning," Jackie recalled for Elizabeth Hayward. "I went quite quickly, in fact, faster than the lap record for this class of car. Driving round there was a big, big thrill. It felt fabulous. At lunchtime Bob said he'd found out what he wanted to know and we set off home again. That was a terrible heartbreak for me because I could have gone on all day. I couldn't imagine why we didn't. But I think I'd made up my mind by then, too." In 1961 McIntyre would test for Ken Tyrrell at Goodwood, again with Stewart in tow. He died in 1962 from injuries suffered in a racing Norton crash.

The Dumbuck customer who so generously loaned his immaculate AC Bristol to the budding road racers was wealthy enthusiast Barry Filer. Preferring not to drive himself for personal and business reasons, Filer was happy to have his cars prepared by Jackie Stewart, who would bring the car to a race or hillclimb, set it up and turn it over to one of Barry's friends to drive. Then one day Filer asked Jackie if he'd like to have a go.

"The first time he asked me, I didn't take it," he said to Hayward. "I was a bit scared; really quite apprehensive – I was not enthusiastic about motor racing anyway. My brother's accidents had affected my mother's health badly and she was very highly strung. If I raced, either she left or I left – that sort of situation. So I turned it down." Filer asked again, however, and Stewart succumbed.

In 1961 Jackie began competing in local events, often at Charterhall, a two-mile airport circuit in the Borders just south of Jim Clark's home town of Duns. In mixed fields he wasn't an immediate winner but he was safe and quick enough to encourage Filer to buy something more interesting for Jackie to race: a Ford-powered Marcos sports car. Built by Jem Marsh to the designs of Frank Costin (Mar-Cos), this was a bizarre-looking contraption that concealed shrewd chassis engineering and a bonded-plywood frame under a coupé body with gullwing doors.

Built as much for racing as for road use, the Marcos came alive in Stewart's sensitive hands. Equipped with a five-speed gearbox for the 1962 season, it was a regular class winner for Jackie at Charterhall that year. Stewart had a taste of bigger cars too. He won in 1961 at Charterhall in Barry Filer's Aston Martin DB4 GT and in 1962 in an E Type Jaguar he co-owned with his brother.

The gorgeous and tractable E Type played a part in another test trip to Cheshire early in 1962. "I didn't know if I had any real ability at that stage," Jackie told journalists Robert Cutter and Bob Fendell, "and, as there was very little real opposition up there, it was difficult to get any comparison. That February, however, Jimmy and I took my father's demonstrator E Jaguar to Oulton Park for some testing. I was both surprised and encouraged to find I was quite close to the times Roy Salvadori had set there the previous September."

"This was to be Jackie's moment of truth," recalled his friend Eric Dymock, who joined the trek to Oulton in the Jaguar, Aston and Marcos. "He had decided that if he was able to reach competitive times at Oulton with any of the cars, he would take up racing seriously. To get some comparative times Jimmy Stewart drove the cars as well. The stopwatch removed all doubt." The younger Stewart was quick enough to be a serious motor racer. In the watershed year of 1962 he cleaned, oiled and put away his guns – except for sports shooting – and picked up his crash helmet.

"I can remember my first couple of seasons in motor racing, when I drove in a nylon short-sleeved shirt, a pair of sandals and a pair of plain slacks, with a crash helmet that I thought looked very nice," he said to Peter Manso. "In large part it was a question of not wanting to appear too much the racing driver because I knew I wasn't. I was an amateur driver and I didn't want to be kidding anyone on." Now those halcyon days were past. The world of driving for dollars beckoned.

Although Jackie's father and brother knew what he was up to, they kept it a secret from his mother. Jackie would race under Barry Filer's name or, in a subterfuge he thought impenetrable, as 'A. N. Other'. But in August 1962 Stewart was a man in the news and the papers blurted out his secret. Jean Stewart learned about her son's clandestine racing career from an article reporting his marriage to a strikingly lovely girl he had known since he was 17, Helen McGregor. They had overcome her parents' reluctance to give their daughter's hand to this rather fast young man. On their honeymoon Jackie adjusted the itinerary so he could turn some laps of the Nürburgring in his company Jaguar 2.4 saloon.

His cover blown, Jackie now competed in the Dumbuck Garage's E Type Jaguar. This brought him numerous successes and in 1963 his first two wins in English events at Rufforth. His handiness in this big car impressed David Murray, whose Ecurie Ecosse racing team had once enjoyed close links with Jaguar, for whom it won the 24 Hours of Le Mans in D Types in 1956 and 1957. Murray's team was struggling with the errant handling of the mid-engined coupés designed and built for Ecurie Ecosse by John Tojeiro. Originally Climax-powered, they now had tuned aluminium-block Buick V-8 engines giving 228 horsepower and driving through – wait for it – a Chevrolet Corvair gearbox.

"I think David telephoned me and asked me to go down to Charterhall and drive the Tojeiro-Buick alongside Tommy Dickson with Jimmy Blumer driving the Cooper Monaco," Jackie told Graham Gauld. Their regular drivers hadn't been able to sort the Tojeiro and the team hoped that Stewart was the man to tame it. His first contact with the car and the team was on that memorable day at Charterhall when, with a dead pedal being hand-crafted to his own specifications, Jackie felt he was at last in motor racing's big-time.

Stewart tried manfully to decipher the handling quirks of the Tojeiro but in fact he created more problems than he solved, simply because he drove the car so much faster than anyone else had. Gearbox quill shafts broke, wheels broke and hub carriers broke under the pressure he applied. That year, said Jackie, "Ecurie Ecosse offered me a place and I finished the season having competed in 23 sports-car races and won 14 of them." Ecosse mechanic Stan Sproat capably chased the flaws in the cars revealed by Stewart's punishing pace.

In addition to victories at Charterhall in 1963, Jackie won races in the ageing and much-cut-about Ecosse Cooper Monaco at Goodwood, Oulton Park and Snetterton. "I owe David Murray of Ecurie Ecosse an awful lot," he reflected. "He gave me the opportunity of being seen on the southern circuits, which would have taken much longer on my own, if indeed I ever would have travelled much in the south."

In 1964 he won again in the Cooper Monaco at Oulton and Goodwood and word was spreading that a very quick new driver was on the scene. "That Ecosse car was the worst Monaco I ever drove," Jimmy Blumer told Doug Nye. It "really was awful, a terrible thing to drive. You could tell just how good Jackie Stewart would be when he was so successful with it."

In January Jackie signed an agreement to drive for Ecurie Ecosse that assured him a minimum retainer of £500 for the season and half of any prize money earned. "They paid my expenses plus a minimum against prize money," Jackie explained to Peter Manso, "and in those days if I won £25 in a weekend, that was a helluva lot more than I was making in my job at the family garage."

Jackie also auditioned and raced Jaguars for John Coombs in 1964, an achievement which he rated "one of the hallmarks of my career because at that time one of my dreams was to drive a John Coombs car. In those days if you had driven for Coombs you knew you had arrived in the big-time. He has bright orange hair and he is a very sarcastic little man, really quite pompous until you get to know him. But after you do, he is one of the most amusing men you could ever wish to know. He is one of the most reliable and one of the most genuine people in racing."

Following his philosophy that he had to drive as many kinds of cars as possible in 1964 so he would know which he was best at driving, Stewart raced a Jaguar 3.8 saloon and a Lotus Cortina for Charles Bridges and a Lotus Elan for Ian Walker. In the Elan he raised eyebrows by keeping up with Jim Clark at Silverstone and beating Peter Arundell at Mallory Park. He practised at Le Mans as a reserve driver, but didn't race, in a Ferrari 330LM and 250GTO. He visited the United States for the first time to win the Marlboro Twelve-Hour race in Maryland co-driving a works Lotus Cortina with Mike Beckwith. And he was racing and winning in the Formula 3 Cooper-BMC for Ken Tyrrell (see Chapter 3) and having his first exposure to Formula 1 in Clark's Lotus.

"In 1964 I drove 26 different cars in 53 races," Jackie summed up, "winning 28 of them. It was a fairly hectic season competing for people like John Coombs, Lotus, the Chequered Flag and Ken Tyrrell." Fraught though it was, this season began to deliver an important message to John Young Stewart: "I started to realise that there was money to be made at racing but I didn't realise there was proper money. What today is proper money. I saw that I could make £8,000 or £9,000 a year and suddenly that was big money – there weren't an awful lot of people making that sort of money who weren't executives or something of the kind.

"We looked after the money very well," Jackie added. "We drove everywhere because we couldn't afford to fly. Just like any young racing driver does." Home base for Jackie and Helen was still Dumbartonshire, first in a flat, then in a bungalow named Clayton House, a clever enough conflation of his accuracy in hitting clay pigeons and the 'ton' that to the British enthusiast is 100 miles per hour. By 1966 he had bought out his parents' interest in the family garage, which was going through a bad patch. He renamed it Jackie Stewart (Dumbuck) Ltd. and kitted out its staff in racing-style overalls.

Although from 1965 Formula 1 would dominate Jackie Stewart's racing life, he remained active in two-seaters. He joined BRM team-mate Graham Hill to drive the turbine-powered Rover-BRM coupé at Le Mans in 1965, competing in the two-litre class. With its fuel supply restricted to avoid aggravating a blade-breakage problem, the Rover-BRM finished tenth overall and third in its class. He returned to Maryland to defend his laurels in the Marlboro Twelve-Hour and led for the first half-hour before retiring with engine failure.

In August 1965 at Brands Hatch Jackie had his first taste of Chevrolet V-8 power in the Lola T70 sports-racer of Team Surtees. He placed third in both heats of the Guards Trophy. Several entries with this car on North America's West Coast in the autumn were unsuccessful, though Stewart learned something of the local driving style. "I saw more accidents than I have seen in Grand Prix and every other type of racing," he told Graham Gauld. "It was monumental, ridiculous – they don't seem to mind bumping each other. They try to out-do each other, baulk each other and don't even look in their mirrors ... what a carry-on!"

Jackie competed in the last two Can-Am races of the 1966 season in a Mecom T70 Lola but failed to finish either. On 30 July 1967, in the midst of his negotiations with Ferrari, he teamed with Chris Amon in an open Ferrari 330P4 to place second to the flying Chaparral in the 500 Miles of Brands Hatch. The result gave Ferrari just the points it needed to win the

Sports Car Constructors' World Championship.

Stewart returned to the Can-Am in July 1970 for a one-off drive at Watkins Glen. He was driving one of the most exotic racing cars ever made, Jim Hall's Chaparral 2J with its separate constant-speed engine powering two huge fans that sucked air from beneath the body and glued the car to the road. "When we introduced the 2J we thought who we'd like to do it, and we thought of Jackie," said Jim Hall. "He agreed to drive it on a one-shot basis at a very reasonable price because he wanted to look at the car and see what it was." It was a very peculiar and underdeveloped sports-racing car with a clutchless torque-converter transmission that required Stewart to learn left-foot braking, which he did with astonishing facility. "This calls for a new sensitivity in getting things co-ordinated," said the Scot, "almost re-learning how to drive."

Stewart qualified third and was chasing the leading McLarens in the same position when various maladies forced the Chaparral's retirement. "I was impressed with him," Hall recalled. "Jackie was fantastic at that time. I was just astounded at his ability. We didn't have enough brakes, we had some other problems with the fans and skirts but he didn't complain about it. He soldiered on and did a hell of a job for us. He drove the bottom off that car."

Jackie was pretty impressed as well, finding the 2J "extraordinary, almost unbelievable. The car has remarkably good adhesion and it's certainly very easy to drive. Notwithstanding the difficulties we've had with the fans pulling in dirt and fouling the belt drives, the car's traction, its ability to brake and go deeply into the corners, is something I've never experienced before in a car this size or bulk."

In the next season's ten-race Can-Am series, with its high-profile prize fund and high-powered sports-racing cars, the dominant orange McLarens faced a series-long challenge from Jackie Stewart in a new Lola T260 with an 8-litre Chevrolet engine. The pooled resources of Goodyear, L&M cigarettes and the Carl Haas team sufficed to persuade Jackie to commit to a gruelling transatlantic commute to drive the newest creation of Lola's Eric Broadley.

In Jim Hall's memorable phrase, Stewart drove the bottom off this car too. He declared his intent by taking pole position in the first race at Mosport. Another track he already knew well was Watkins Glen, where he also took pole position. Jackie won twice with the Lola, at St. Jovite in Canada and at Mid-Ohio, a bumpy track he detested, and twice placed second in a 1971 season littered with retirements. He ranked third in the final Can-Am points behind champion Peter Revson and Denny Hulme.

The powerful Lola was a veritable bear to drive. More than 20 years later the experience came in handy when one of Paul Stewart's Formula 3000 drivers stepped out of his Reynard at Spa, calling it "undriveable". Jackie's rejoinder was quick: "Undriveable? Listen, I drove the Can-Am Lola in 1971!" He accepted a better Can-Am ride in 1972, a seat in an orange works McLaren, but at the last minute was ordered to give it up by the doctor treating his duodenal ulcer.

Commenting on his Lola-driving effort at Road Atlanta in 1971, where he set a record-breaking race lap with a time quicker than Denny Hulme's pole-setting practice lap after having to pit twice with tyre troubles, Jackie said, "I don't believe you should give up in any race. I think the moment you give up, you start getting used to the idea. I've always driven as hard as I can when I'm in it." Hall and Haas will testify to that. So will the talent spotters who shrewdly saw the Stewart potential for speed in single-seaters.

The Ford-powered plywood-chassised Marcos created by Jem Marsh and Frank Costin is agile and quick enough to show off the skills of a budding racing driver in his first serious season, 1961. At Charterhall Jackie Stewart is harrying the Porsche Carrera of Gordon Durham.

72
G 128

40
G 128

Jem Marsh personally delivered the brand-new Marcos (£795 in kit form) to Scottish enthusiast Barry Filer, who bought it for Jackie to race. At Charterhall in 1961 Filer, in white jumper, hacksaws some added suspension clearance (above left) and Jackie personally sees to the race numbers (above right). Stewart (72 below) is in heavy Charterhall traffic including an AC Ace, Lotus Elite and the E Type Jaguar of his friend and Dumbuck Garage customer Ronnie Morrison. Jackie also competes in Scotland's Rest and Be Thankful hillclimb (facing page).

REDEX
ADDITIVE
6

Stewart thought he had reached the apogee of his ambitions in motor racing when David Murray asked him to drive the Ecurie Ecosse Tojeiro coupé, a purpose-built albeit flawed sports-racing car. At Brands Hatch in July 1964 (preceding pages) Graham Gauld catches him removing his helmet and preparing to brief fedora-hatted David Murray on the coupé in Ford-powered form. A beharnessed Jackie (facing page) chats with Jim Clark, whose hand is just visible; his racing suit can be seen beneath a sports jacket. Stewart races to third at Brands (top and middle). At Charterhall in 1963 (bottom) he leads team-mate Tommy Dickson, both Tojeiros powered by Buick.

The methodical Jackie's aim early in his career is to drive as many kinds of car as possible so he'll know which sort he drives best. This plan is frustrated by his obvious speed in everything including Hugh Patrick's Jaguar 3.8 at Charterhall (above), a works Lotus-Cortina at Brands (below) and (facing page) a John Coombs E Type Jaguar in which he leads from the start at Brands in 1964 from David Piper's Ferrari GTO and the Shelby Cobras of Jack Sears and Roy Salvadori. Sears wins with Stewart second.

ARMSTRONG
CHAMPION
SUPER S
CASTROL
CASTROL

BRM team-mates Jackie Stewart and Graham Hill share the turbine-powered Rover-BRM at Le Mans in 1965, competing as a 2-litre Prototype (above). They place 10th overall and second in class.

Stewart and Hill team up again (right) to drive an aluminium-bodied Ford GT40 at Sebring in 1966 for Briton Alan Mann. They hold fourth early in the race but strike engine trouble and retire.

24
P

The team that came close to being Enzo Ferrari's Formula 1 pairing for 1968 – Chris Amon and Jackie Stewart – shares a 4-litre Ferrari P4 in the 500-mile race at Brands Hatch on 30 July 1967, which is won by the Chevrolet-powered Chaparral 2F. By placing second in the Brands Hatch race ahead of the best Porsche, Stewart and Amon secure the FIA Group 6 Constructors' Championship for Ferrari by a margin of just two points. Italian sporting magazine Autosprint *shows Jackie its appreciation.*

DAGER
6

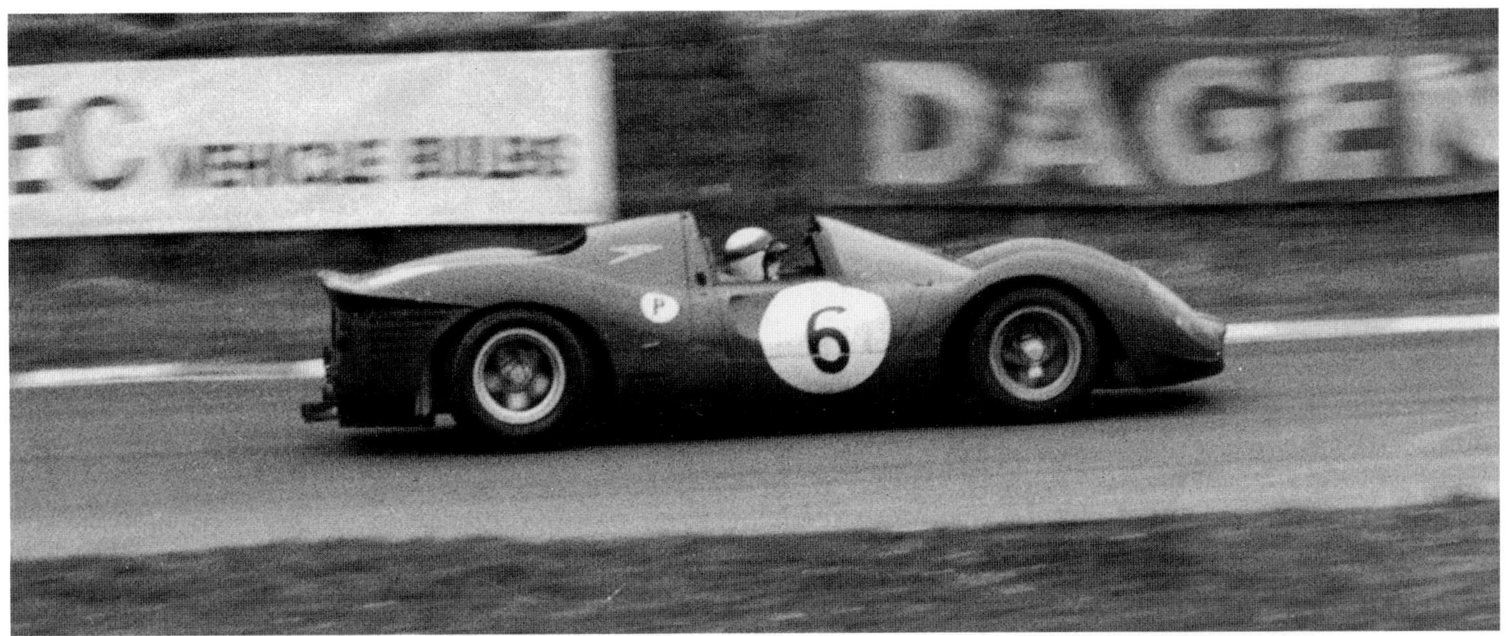

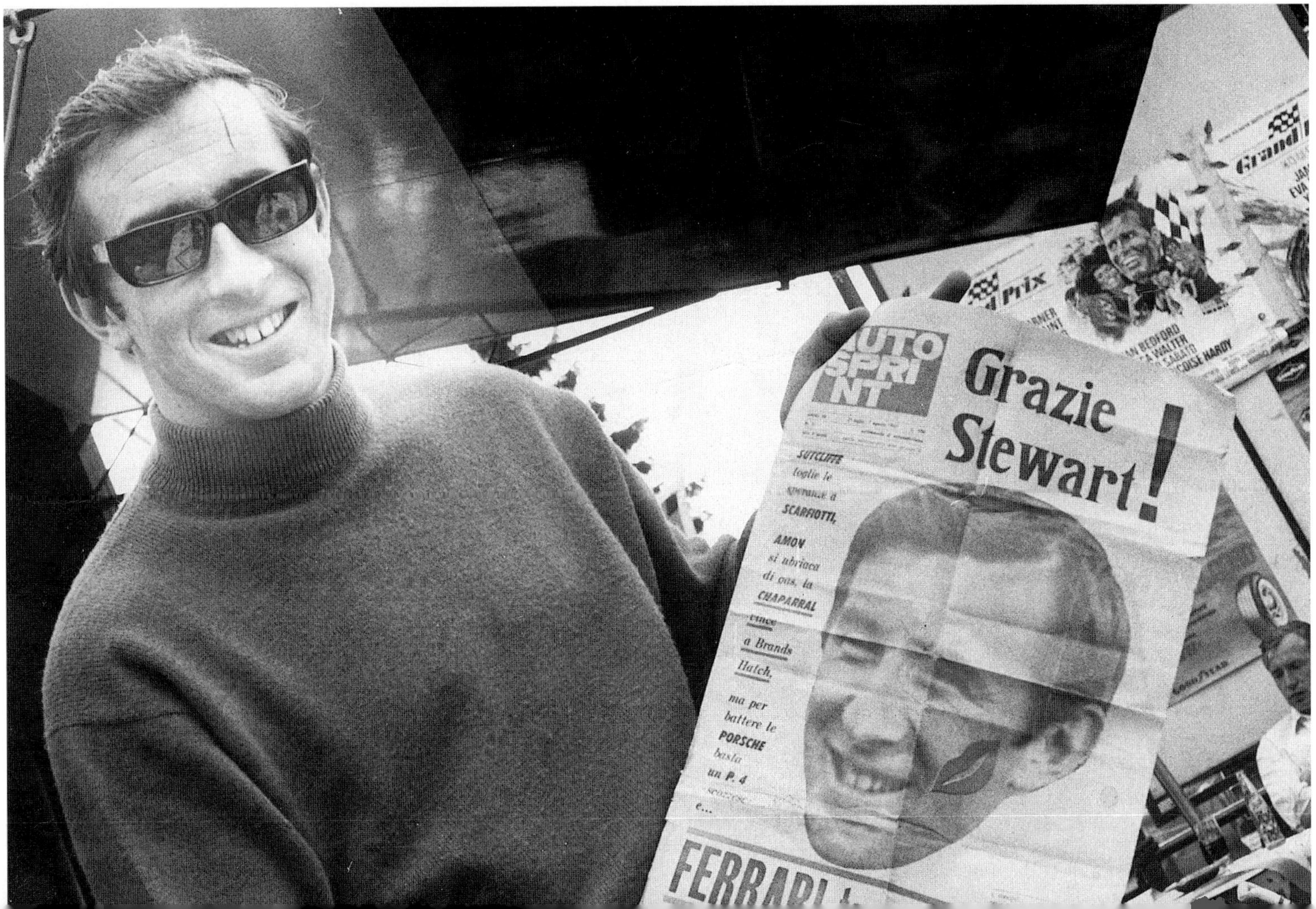
AUTO SPRINT
Grazie Stewart!
SUTCLIFFE toglie le speranze a SCARFIOTTI,
AMON si ubriaca di gas, la CHAPARRAL vince a Brands Hatch,
ma per battere le PORSCHE basta un P. 4
e...
FERRARI

"How do I find myself in Upper New York state driving this extraordinary car?" That seems to sum up Jackie's expression in the cockpit of the awesome Chaparral 2J (preceding pages), which he races for its Texan creator Jim Hall at Watkins Glen in 1970.

Hall knows his radical 2J Chaparral with its twin fans sucking it to the track is underdeveloped, but he wants to race it before others twig its advantages. Stewart drives it with total commitment before being forced to retire from the Glen Can-Am race.

66
Firestone

Jackie is signed to partner Denny Hulme (right above) in the all-conquering McLaren Can-Am team for 1972, but at the last minute he withdraws on doctor's orders and is replaced by Peter Revson (centre above). In the 2J he practises with Richard Attwood's Porsche 917 at the Glen in 1970 (below).

Eight litres of Chevrolet in the Lola T260 make for a volatile package in the 1971 Can-Am series, as Jackie points out to designer Eric Broadley (above). L&M gets its money's worth from Stewart, who joins team owner Carl Haas to show the Lola to President Richard Nixon (left below) at the White House.

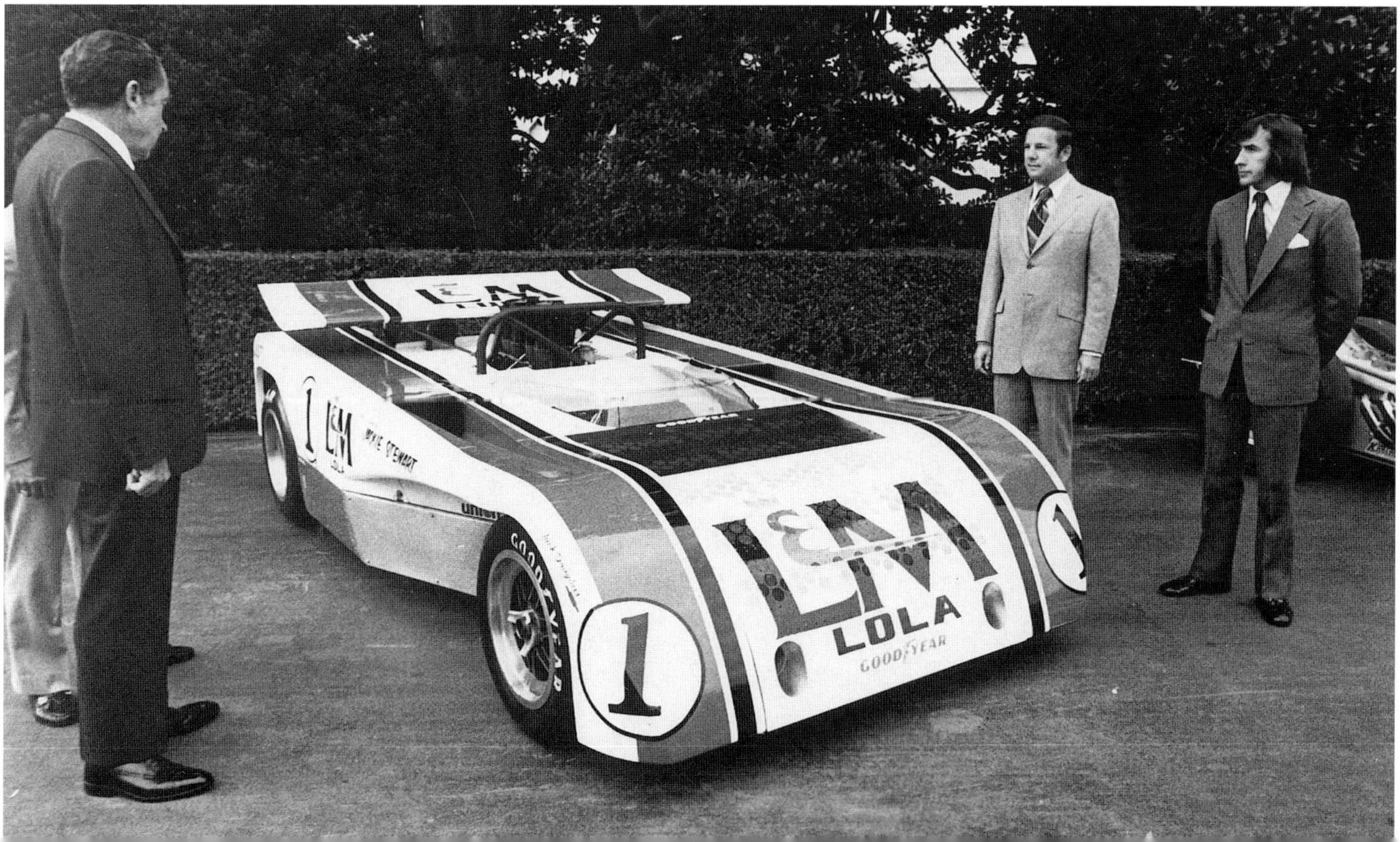

ESSO
C'EST
Englebert
Englebert
LONGLIFE
LONGLIFE
BP

CHAPTER 3

That great new driver

"It was rather strange and amusing that in 1964 I should find myself in the same position as Bob McIntyre on a cold March morning, arriving at Goodwood to try Ken's Formula 3 Cooper." Three years earlier Jackie had been asked along to Goodwood by motorcycle racer McIntyre, who was being given a test by Ken Tyrrell.

Stewart on his 1961 Goodwood visit: "That day I would have given my right arm to drive the Formula Junior Cooper-BMC which Ken was running at the time and I remember mentioning to him that I had just started to race, having driven a roadgoing Porsche around Oulton Park!" But both Jackie's arms remained firmly in place. In fact, when Tyrrell's 1964 invitation was issued he was not all that sure that he wanted to risk the big-time.

Moving into single-seaters would be a major step for Jackie Stewart. As long as he carried on driving sports cars he could rationalise his racing as an agreeable promotional activity for the family garage and motor sales agency, where he was working, and a welcome relief from the tension of trapshooting, which was his sport and hobby combined. But anyone stepping into a single-seater racing car had to admit that he had certain ambitions, that he was not just weekending at the wheel.

"I hadn't really wanted ever to drive a single-seater car," Stewart told Barrie Gill. "I thought they were far too dangerous. I was only racing for fun anyway – in E Types. That was quite enough for me." Had Jackie forgotten his hankering in 1961 when he accompanied McIntyre to Goodwood? Well, testing one was not the same as racing one, was it?

"Ken offered me this test drive and I suddenly changed my mind. I don't know to this day what made me change my mind," he said to Gill, wondering later at an occurrence which is not all that common in this man's life. "Perhaps it was a hunger for success ... and, I must confess, a need constantly to test myself."

This could be any one of 11 tracks across Europe in 1964 but in fact it is Rouen in France, where Bernard Cahier freezes the flag-fall for another Formula 3 victory for Jackie Stewart in his Tyrrell-entered Cooper-BMC.

The mind-change wasn't achieved all that suddenly. The phone lines from Dumbarton hummed. Jackie Stewart quizzed friends for their opinions, among them David Murray of Ecurie Ecosse and journalist Graham Gauld. At the nexus of calls from both Tyrrell and Jackie was another Stewart, his brother Jimmy, who was eight years older and had himself been a promising driver before a serious crash ended his career in 1955.

Biographers tend to dismiss Jimmy Stewart's time on the tracks in the 1950s as "ill-starred attempts at a racing career," as did *Time* magazine. But in the years before British racing cars were on top of the world's game the chubby-faced Jimmy was a feared competitor driving for David Murray's Scottish racing team, Ecurie Ecosse, in a C Type Jaguar and Cooper-Bristol single-seater. Based in Edinburgh, the Ecurie was not far from the Stewart family home on the outskirts of Glasgow.

An invitation to drive at Le Mans for Aston Martin in 1954 turned sour when the appalling aerodynamics of Jimmy's DB3S coupé led to a bad crash and a broken elbow. He bounced back and signed a Jaguar works driving contract for the 1955 season. Jaguar planned to pair him with Mike Hawthorn at Le Mans. But he injured the same arm again at the Nürburgring that spring and, on his doctor's advice, stood down from the cockpit. Ivor Bueb filled the seat instead and won Le Mans with Hawthorn.

"Perhaps the best assessment of Jimmy Stewart as a racing driver comes from his rival in the early days of Ecurie Ecosse, Ian Stewart," wrote Graham Gauld of an unrelated member of the Clan Stewart: "'There are lucky drivers and unlucky drivers and Jimmy was the match if not better than his brother but I think Jackie was lucky and Jimmy wasn't ... it's a magic thing, isn't it?'" Come to think of it, "ill-starred" wasn't a bad description.

Whatever others may have thought, Jackie Stewart was well aware of his older brother's achievements and indeed of his reputation. He had joined the family to watch Jimmy competing against the Ascaris, Bonettos, Mosses, Hawthorns and Villoresis of his day, running a Cooper-Bristol in sixth place at the 1953 British Grand Prix before a wheel literally fell off. "I used to think of them as Gods," Jackie admitted. "They appeared something very special indeed. I couldn't even begin to think that one day I would be in amongst them."

Whether or not others would measure Jackie against his brother, *he* certainly would. Jimmy had been named one of Britain's most promising young drivers by the editors of *Motor Racing*. "There was no point in my going racing if I wasn't going to be any good at it," Jackie mused to Chris McCall. "And anyway, I didn't want people to say I was just Jimmy Stewart's little brother."

In 1963 Jimmy Stewart's little brother had been chalking up quite a record of his own in various sports and sports-racing cars for Ecurie Ecosse, and word of his successes had reached the generously-dimensioned ears of a tall, buck-toothed timber harvester and transporter whose business was based in wooden sheds near Ockham in Surrey. R. Kenneth Tyrrell, a gamekeeper's son, had started Tyrrell Brothers Ltd. with his brother and in the meantime had become besotted with motorsports. He would bring to it the same high standards and determination he bestowed on his timber company.

Ken Tyrrell started as a driver in 1952 at the age of 28, racing the popular 500cc Cooper-Norton single-seaters and graduating to the Formula 2 Coopers. "I had a bad accident at Goodwood," Tyrrell recalled, "and after that I never seemed capable of reproducing the form I had shown previously. By accident almost I loaned the Formula 2 Cooper I was using at the time to a friend who did very well in it. That experience pointed the way for me as an entrant of race cars rather than as a driver." If Tyrrell could not reach the standard he had set for himself as a driver, he would endeavour to do so as an entrant and team manager.

Ken Tyrrell's close association with Cooper Cars continued with the management of Formula 2 and

Formula Junior teams for Cooper. In 1963 he formed the Tyrrell Racing Organisation to run, very successfully, Cooper-BMC Formula Junior single-seaters with an outstanding new American driver, Timmy Mayer. Together they were gearing up for a 1964 campaign in the new one-litre Formula 3 category, like Formula Junior still using stock-based engines, for which Cooper was building a delectably low, slim racing car, the T72.

Tragically, young Mayer was killed in a crash at the Longford track in Tasmania on the last day of February 1964 and Tyrrell was without a driver. Because officially 'graded' top-level drivers were excluded from Formula 3 in order to help newcomers gain a foothold on the racing ladder, Ken had to look elsewhere for a pilot. "The conditions we operated under forced us to search for new drivers all the time," he said, "and really it only takes a degree of common sense to see who is good and who is not." This was an attribute that Ken Tyrrell had in spades.

"It was while discussing drivers with Robin McKay, the Goodwood track manager, that Stewart's name was raised," wrote Doug Nye. "McKay had seen him equalling the Sussex circuit's sports car record in a tired old Cooper Monaco belonging to Ecurie Ecosse." Ken had forgotten the young Scot who had tugged at his sleeve three years earlier. The phone-call flurry was triggered when Tyrrell called Jimmy Stewart and was assured that the younger brother, then 24, was "very serious" about his racing.

Not only was a driver being tested on that day at Goodwood early in 1964; the new Formula 3 Cooper-BMC was being tested as well. What a gorgeous little car it was, with its inboard front springing, dark-green paintwork and the two white stripes down the nose that marked an official Cooper car. Its BMC-tuned A-Series engine pumped out 88 horsepower at 7,750rpm. John Cooper himself was on hand with works Formula 1 driver Bruce McLaren, who was to check and validate the new chassis and set a bogey time, which he did with his usual confident skill.

Then it was Stewart's turn. As he settled into the sloped-back seat he knew the occasion was special. He was accustomed to doing his best when tested. But he reminded himself that he already had a secure place at his family's garage and that he was enjoying his drives with the Ecurie Ecosse. If this didn't work out he wouldn't be bereft. Still, trying a single-seater was a new assessment of his abilities and he liked rising to a challenge. He listened closely to the guidance, indeed warnings, he was being given by Ken Tyrrell.

The snug cockpit reassured, as did the tiny steering wheel with its quick response. Accelerating away, Jackie realised that the Cooper's performance didn't match that of the big-engined sports cars he'd been racing but the handling and braking were a revelation. He experienced "the exhilaration of driving such a precise machine. It seemed to do everything I wanted it to do." He knew Goodwood well, and after only three laps he was still getting settled when Tyrrell flagged him to stop. What was the matter?

Stewart had already equalled Bruce McLaren's lap time. "I was frightened, so I called him in," said Tyrrell, concerned that the youngster was driving well over his own limit and heading for a smash. While the team manager lectured the recruit, McLaren in a "this is ridiculous" frame of mind returned to the track and carved two seconds off his time. "Then blow me, Stewart went out and beat those times too," recalled an astonished but delighted Tyrrell.

Encouraged by an equally-impressed John Cooper, Ken Tyrrell signed the young Scot for the 1964 Formula 3 season. He had a shrewd plan as well. If Jackie would agree to allocate ten percent of his future earnings to Tyrrell, the latter suggested, he would advance the substantial sum of £10,000 to Stewart. But the young Scot was equally canny. If this experienced team manager thought so well of his prospects, reasoned Jackie, he should probably steer clear of that commitment – a decision he has never had reason to regret.

In 1964 Stewart had confirmation that Tyrrell and money were not easily parted. "The only real drawback to working with Ken," he said later, "is his unerring aptitude for picking the worst hotels in the world. In our Formula 3 days we stayed in one for a race at Rouen which had naked light bulbs and the plaster falling off the walls. I spent the entire night throwing rocks at the rats in the courtyard."

Their first race together was at Norfolk's Snetterton on 14 March 1964. It was early days for a new racing formula; no one knew the form. And here was one of the most desirable rides going, in a Tyrrell Cooper, snagged by a cheeky Scottish upstart of whom few had even heard. "There were people just waiting to see him fail," Ken Tyrrell recalled for Barrie Gill. "They were bitterly disappointed!"

Race day was as windy and wet as only Norfolk can be. The rain intensified for the Formula 3 event, the last on the card. Lowering clouds and the approach of dusk cut the race length from 20 laps to ten. At flagfall Stewart rocketed into the distance and at the end of the first 2.7-mile lap had a 14-second lead. "He just vanished in a cloud of spray," said Tyrrell. "Most of the time he seemed to spend looking back to see where the others were. He won by about half a minute." Actually it was 44 seconds.

"Even to this day I don't know where the hell the rest of them got to," Jackie told Graham Gauld. "I don't know why they were so slow, for it wasn't as impossible as all that. There were loads of puddles and you aquaplaned at every corner, but as long as you were careful you could drive reasonably quickly." Cyril Posthumus called it "an impressive walkover" for J. Y. Stewart, whose virtuosity also made it the "least interesting race of the day."

This accusation would be heard often in 1964. Stewart and Tyrrell went on to win 11 out of their 13 Formula 3 entries that year. Critics muttered that the Tyrrell operation was a thinly-disguised Cooper works entry with its BMC-tuned engines competing in a category that was meant for impecunious privateers. Nevertheless Jackie shone, and was called "very promising" and "that great new driver" by the press. It was all Ken Tyrrell could do to convince team-mate Warwick Banks that his team's two Coopers were identical.

"Formula 3 taught me to drive as smoothly as I possibly could," Jackie told Robert Cutter and Bob Fendell. "You must be smooth. If you start being erratic and hairy in a Formula 3 car, you do nothing but slow yourself down. Ken taught me all about gear ratios when I drove for him in Formula 3. I came to his team a raw boy from the Highlands, unused to the professional approach in motor racing. Ken had the car set up for me and educated me in the selection of a high gear for slip-streaming circuits, or the most suitable intermediate gear for pulling away from an important corner."

Ken was willing to teach and Jackie was an eager and able scholar, perhaps one of the quickest learners motor racing has ever seen. Jackie was and is a world-class talker but unlike many in his league he also had a facility for listening to those whose knowledge he felt could contribute to his progress in a sport which, at this level, was completely new to him.

Other teams quickly noted the obvious class of Tyrrell's discovery. Ron Harris, a racing-besotted film distributor who was then running the Lotus team in the Formula 2 class for one-litre four-cylinder pure racing engines, invited Jackie to drive in races that didn't conflict with Formula 3. In his first outing for Harris he was second to Denny Hulme at the challenging Clermont-Ferrand track and later that year at Snetterton, the scene of his dramatic debut, he won outright for the Harris team. He also raced BRM-powered Formula 2 Coopers for Tyrrell, but this was a much less successful model.

Here, at the higher level in which drivers like Hulme and Rindt were competing, Jackie was learning more – "especially about racecraft as such – the biding of your time or going all out, for example. In Formula 3 if you slackened up slightly, you could still put the steam on and get back up there. In Formula 2 you couldn't do that. The competition was so strong that if you slackened someone would pass you and you just couldn't catch up again unless he slackened.

You had to concentrate hard all the time."

Jackie Stewart was enjoying great success but his natural wariness left him wondering when he would strike the buffers of his racing career. To Graham Gauld in June 1964 he said, "If I establish myself this year as being versatile and able to drive various types of car, when it comes to next year I am going to have it clearly stuck in my mind which cars I drive best." Including his Formula 3 successes he won two dozen races that year, confirming his talent at the wheel. Several people were sure they knew what Stewart would drive best: Formula 1 cars.

"As early as April 1964 Tim Parnell asked me to drive a Formula 1 Lotus for him in races where Mike Hailwood was absent through motorcycle commitments," Jackie recalled. "I remember he asked me this in the paddock at Aintree where I was driving a Formula 3 car and I nearly fell through the railings at Tatts Corner. I had only driven in one or two single-seater races and it was all a bit over-awing, so I decided to say 'no' because of my inexperience."

By this time Jackie had another source of valuable advice about both race driving and life in general: fellow Scot Jim Clark. Fresh from his World Championship with Team Lotus in 1963, Clark had a London base at John Whitmore's flat which he arranged for Jackie to share during the busier parts of the racing season. Clark introduced Stewart to some of the necessities of racing life, such as a knowledgeable team of lawyers and accountants. Jackie paid close attention to every tip; he called it "getting the clues" and he was good at it.

Clark stage-managed Jackie's first taste of Formula 1 that summer of 1964 at the British Grand Prix meeting. Stewart was racing a few other cars that weekend: a Lotus Cortina, an Ecurie Ecosse Tojeiro-Buick coupé and a lightweight E Type Jaguar entered by John Coombs. Between races he frequented the Brands tea-room, where he spent some time "getting the clues" from the man who would be World Champion for Ferrari that season, John Surtees.

Jim Clark approached Colin Chapman, who was not uninterested in a possible new driver signing, to ask whether the Lotus chief would let his flatmate have a go in one of his Formula 1 cars. It was an open secret that BRM had spent an evening romancing the young Stewart aboard ship on the Seine at the previous meeting at Rouen. Cooper was also interested in Jackie, of course, but the Cooper team was no longer the force it had been in Jack Brabham's two Championship years with them. Lotus, where Jackie could be Clark's team-mate, was the obvious alternative to BRM.

Chapman worked out a scheme for the track marshals to stay at their posts after official practice at Brands so Stewart could try Clark's Lotus. It was sunny at the Kent circuit in July as Jackie squirmed into Clark's seat and absorbed the 'clues' from the acknowledged master.

Accelerating out of the pits and over the brow into Paddock Corner, Jackie found the power of the Climax V-8 not awesome by his standards but the shift pattern of the ZF gearbox was peculiar. Shifting problems soon provoked a spin and a very second-hand Climax V-8 and the outing ended after only three laps with a suspected dropped valve. Clark left Brands that year with the winner's trophy, won in his re-engined Lotus, and Jackie left with an offer of £4,000 and plenty of test-driving time in 1965 from BRM. It was an offer he would accept.

At the end of the 1965 season Jackie raced a Lola T70 in two North American races for Texan team owner John Mecom, Jr. He stayed on in November to visit Indiana's Crucible of Speed, the 2½-mile Indianapolis Motor Speedway. Mecom wheeled out one of his new Lola-Ford Indy cars and put Stewart behind its wheel. Jackie's smooth style was made to order for the huge track with its four similar yet bafflingly different corners and he was soon lapping at better than 150mph. The man and the track were well mated.

The Mecom team entered BRM team-mates Graham Hill and Jackie Stewart in Lola-Fords for the Indy 500-mile race in 1966. These were the palmy years when British racing-car technology, led by Dan Gurney with Colin Chapman and Lotus, was invading the American scene and towing European drivers in its wake. Luckily avoiding a first-lap crash involving 14 cars, the Mecom Lolas figured strongly in the drama of that year's 500.

In spite of stalling the engine on one of his pit stops, Jackie took the lead on lap 147 when Lloyd Ruby retired. He began cheerfully clicking off the leading laps, each worth $150. But on lap 192, only 20 miles from the chequered flag, "the oil pressure fell away and the engine began to seize." He flipped off the ignition and parked on the infield grass, then pushed the Lola to the pits. Graham Hill went through to win in the other Mecom Lola ahead of Jim Clark in second.

"I felt a slight tinge of disappointment," Jackie reflected afterward, "but I wasn't angry. You can never get annoyed with these things because there is nothing you can do about it. I must have dropped, personally, $130–140,000. That's a lot of money for an American but think of it from a Scotsman's point of view! But I had led Indianapolis, never having been there before. So, therefore, I had a certain amount of elation from having led the race and thinking, 'Well, these bastards will at least know I've been here.'" Indeed, the difference between winner Hill's $156,297 purse and Stewart's winnings of $25,267 was a hefty $131,030.

Jackie had the satisfaction of beating "those bastards" at the end of the 1966 season in Japan. The American racers decamped *en masse* in a chartered Boeing 707, more than 100 strong, to the Fuji International road circuit at the foot of the dormant volcano and raced over 200 miles in their usual counter-clockwise direction over a shortened version of the road course.

No first-lap crash was needed to demoralise and decimate the opposition, although the track's peculiarities put paid to the engines of Jim Clark and Mario Andretti. Stewart won pole position and Graham Hill was next to him in the other Mecom Lola. Jackie was by now a seasoned road-racer whose skills brought him victory in Japan; only Bobby Unser's Eagle-Ford was on the same lap at the finish.

Jackie Stewart raced again at Indianapolis for Mecom and Lola in 1967 but with less success; although he worked his way up to a comfortable third place he had to retire on the 169th lap with engine failure. Nevertheless he earned $12,796 for his team. As Jackie said, a race with a purse the size of Indy's had a special appeal for a Scotsman. An injury to his right wrist made him miss the 500 in 1968 and in 1969 he said, "I hope to be back at Indianapolis. I just didn't come up with a good Indy ride this year."

The Indy 500, then, was and remained unfinished business for Jackie Stewart. In the meantime, however, he made his mark in Formula 1 in no uncertain manner. BRM gave him plenty of testing time – and chances to win races.

Nineteen-sixty-four is the season that launches a close relationship between no-nonsense experienced team owner Ken Tyrrell and stubborn eager racing driver Jackie Stewart. They will argue their way to a decade of success.

Graham Gauld risks his camera to record Stewart's debut race for the Tyrrell team at a rainy Snetterton in March 1964. Jackie boots up in Tyrrell's van and adds helmet, visor and wet suit. A last mirror check (above right) is made before a first lap (right) that leaves the others wondering where he went. He is simply the class of the class in the semi-works Cooper in 1964 (overleaf).

30

120

In the years when the great drivers also compete in lesser formulae Stewart is active in Formula 2, forging his relationship with the new French Matra Automobile company. In a Matra (above) he chases Brabham and leader Hulme in the Easter Monday race at Goodwood in 1966 before spinning with a stuck throttle and taking over Ickx's car to place sixth. He and his F2 Matra-Ford are beaten by close friend Jochen Rindt (no. 4) in the Guards Trophy at Brands in 1967, and at Pau in April 1969 (overleaf). Jackie races a Brabham BT30 for John Coombs at Crystal Palace in 1970 (below) and starts from pole to win his heat and the final and set fastest lap.

NLOP
DUNLO
BP
BP
12
WINKELMANN RACING
4
Firestone

MATRA F2
elf
JACKIE STEWAR
DUNLOP
elf

QUIPE MATRA ELF
6
FERODO

Stewart's first laps in a Formula 1 car are in a 1½-litre Lotus Climax after official practice for the 1964 British Grand Prix at Brands Hatch (below). He tries it for size (left) and "gets the clues" from Jim Clark (above). Shifting problems lead to a spin and a distinctly second-hand Lotus.

Jackie is in the vanguard of the second wave of the British invasion of the Indianapolis 500, testing a new Ford-powered Lola T80 at the Speedway in 1965 with ace mechanic George Bignotti and Lola's Eric Broadley (left to right above) and joining Andy Granatelli, Jim Clark and Art Pollard (left to right below) at the 500 in 1967. Stewart led until retiring eight laps from the end of the 1966 race (overleaf), handing the win to Graham Hill in a sister car.

STP
43

BOWES
SPECIAL

For a home-loving Scotsman the 1966 season has many surprises. Jackie Stewart is an Indianapolis, Indiana railbird (above) between team owner John Mecom (left) and racer Parnelli Jones. In the Lola-Ford he clicks off one of his 40 leading laps at Indy in 1966 (below), each worth a tidy $150.

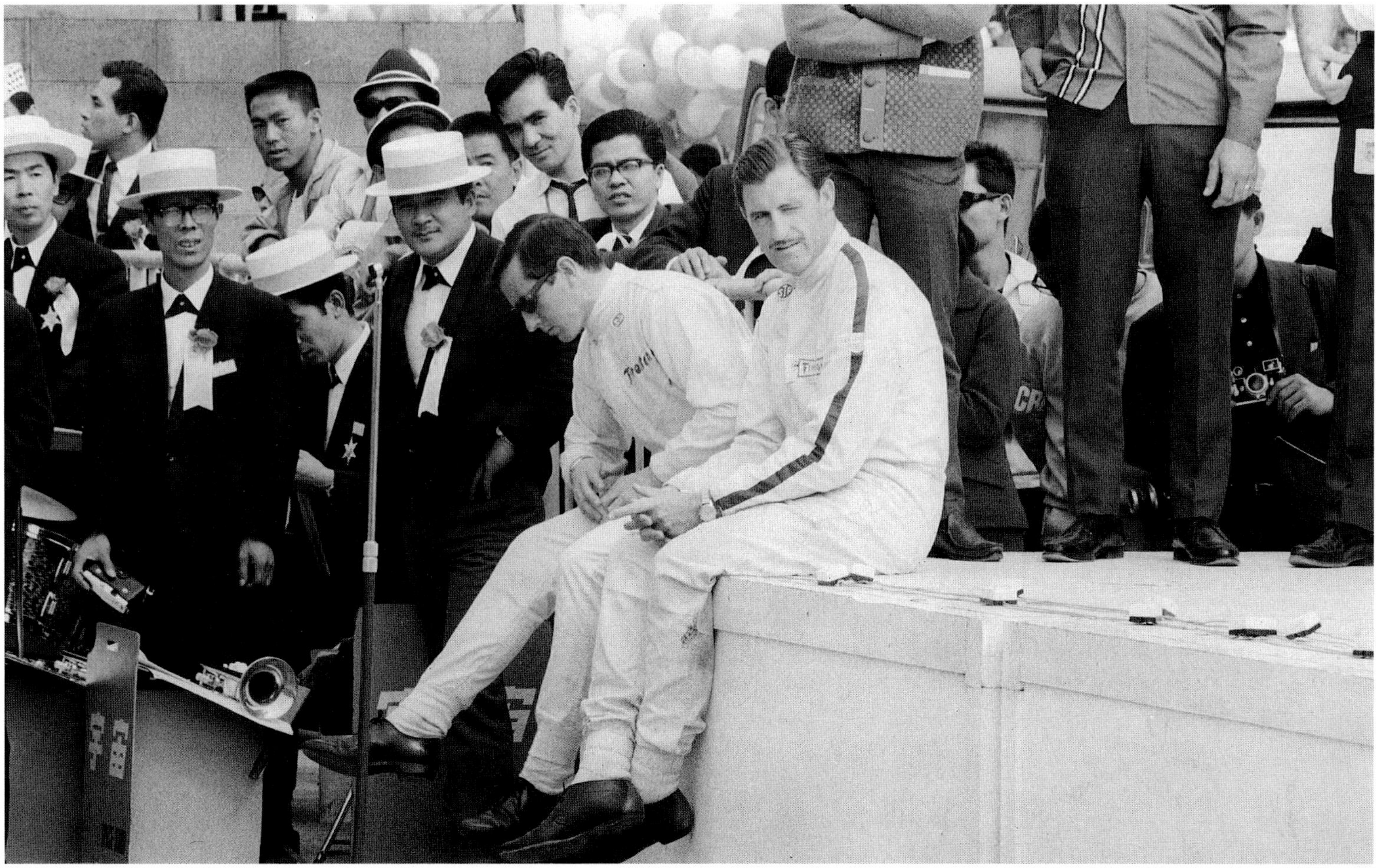

The atmosphere is altogether different at the end of 1966 at Fuji, Japan, where Stewart and Graham Hill join the brass band for pre-race festivities (above). Jackie comes home the winner in his Mecom Lola (below) after 200 miles on a track generously strewn with Speedi-Dri absorbent powder after numerous oil spills (overleaf).

Moteurs LE MAGAZINE DU SPORT AUTOMOBILE
DYNAMOS DEMARREURS
PAR
DUNLOP
TOTAL
4

CHAPTER 4

British racing motorist

With Ferrari and, at that time, Honda, Britain's BRM was among the few constructors of complete racing cars competing in Formula 1. It traced its origins as British Racing Motors to an ill-fated effort to harness the skills of Britain's car and components producers to the building of a world-beating $1^1/2$-litre 16-cylinder Grand Prix car in the 1940s.

The prime mover behind BRM's creation was Raymond Mays, the founder of ERA in his salad days of the 1930s and as great a name in British motor racing as Jackie Stewart was to become. But in 1964 at Rouen when Jackie Stewart was being introduced to Raymond Mays, who took care of driver contracts for the BRM team, there was only one small hitch: Mays had never heard of Stewart.

This was an awkward moment for BRM chief engineer Tony Rudd, who had talent-spotted Stewart and was counting on the silver-tongued Mays to help lure JYS into the clutches of BRM. Fortunately Jean Stanley came to his rescue. Married to author Louis Stanley, Jean was the sister of Alfred Owen of Rubery Owen, the big motor industry supplier that had taken over the BRM racing-car enterprise, complete with its manufactory in the shade of the Mays family home in Bourne, Lincolnshire, in October of 1952. Subsequently BRMs were fielded by the Owen Racing Organisation.

Jean Stanley's personal commitment to, and interest in, motorsports was to stand BRM in good stead. It did so that day at Rouen when she helped a young Scot feel more at home at BRM which was, after all, one of the most exalted Formula 1 houses after Graham Hill's World Championship in 1962. Graham was second on points in 1963 and would be again in 1964 (just one point shy of John Surtees).

Rudd was an important factor favouring a pro-BRM decision, Jackie felt: "Tony Rudd has been actively involved in motor racing since the days of Bira and he has accumulated an enormous wealth of knowledge.

Jackie Stewart leads five laps of the second World Championship Grand Prix he contests for BRM at Monaco on 30 May 1965, under the eye of Jesse Alexander's camera. He finishes third after an oil-provoked spin and recovery.

He is one of the very quiet operators who goes about his job very efficiently."

Rudd had to compete against Team Lotus, where Jackie could have a drive with Jim Clark in a car of known competitiveness. But Chapman, assuming that this gave him an advantage, penny-pinched the negotiations. Stewart: "BRM had offered me no more money than Lotus. It was £4,000. But the difference was that Lotus had doubled and redoubled their figure to match BRM's, and I felt dubious about accepting something which they had had such difficulty in arriving at."

There was another factor, of course, and Jackie acknowledged it: "I knew Jimmy Clark had a competitive car and probably the best car, and I respected him as the best driver too. I wasn't sure that if put in a Lotus I could have kept up with him. I might not have been able to beat him. It's always a thought because when somebody is beating you, you want to know why." By not joining Lotus, the canny Stewart avoided the demoralisation that he might have reaped from such a relationship. In Formula 1 the two Scots never competed on the same track in the same kinds of cars at the same time.

The experienced Tony Rudd also allayed some of the fears that might have beset a driver new to Grand Prix racing. "When I first went to the BRM works at Bourne," Jackie recalled, "Tony Rudd said to me, 'We've got five Formula 1 cars, two of them for Graham Hill, one for you and two other cars, one for development and one that you can use to get acclimatised. You can have it as many times as you want, do as many laps as you like on as many circuits as you like, take the mechanics along and drive it to your heart's content.' What more could any new boy ask for? Naturally I took full advantage of this offer."

Ironically, before Jackie joined BRM he had already raced a Lotus in Formula 1 – in the non-Championship Rand Grand Prix at Kyalami, run in two heats on 12 December 1964. Jim Clark had injured a disc while horsing around throwing snowballs at Cortina d'Ampezzo, and Colin Chapman drafted Speedy Scot the Younger to take his place. He promptly qualified Clark's Lotus 33 on the pole next to team-mate Mike Spence.

At the start of the first heat at Kyalami the left half-shaft of Stewart's Lotus neatly sheared and the right one twisted, leaving Jackie on the grid and very lucky to be missed by the departing field. Graham Hill won in a Brabham-BRM with Spence second. Repaired just five minutes before the second-heat start, the Lotus-Climax was now right at the back of the grid. After two laps Jackie was fifth, after five laps third and on the sixth lap he smoothly raced by his remaining rivals, including Graham Hill, into a lead which he never relinquished.

Racing the Lotus was edifying for Stewart, as Philip Turner reported: "The Lotus impressed him greatly. It was delightful to drive, for it could be put just where the driver wanted and could be twitched straight at 130–140mph with great ease should it slide. Its traction was fantastic, just as though it was putting the power down six inches beneath the road surface."

The BRM V-8, when Jackie came to test it, was horsepower of a different colour. It was "stiff and unyielding", set up to cope with Graham Hill's attacking style. Hill liked a rigid set-up that he could dominate; Stewart preferred a supple chassis that he could control. "I always ask for understeer on my car," he said in 1965, "because I'm very conscious of coming out of corners quickly – I don't go into corners quickly but I like to get away from them fast."

With a touch of understeer the driver can accelerate hard while gently trimming the front wheels to exit the corner just before the surface turns from black to green. The disadvantage, of course, is that if the driver misjudges the distance he needs to complete that manoeuvre he runs out of road as Jackie found on a fast corner at the Nürburgring in 1965: "I thought I'd lead the car out – you know, take off a bit of lock and use up as much of the road as possible – but unfortunately in this case I used up about six inches too much! On any other circuit this would have been all right, but not at the 'Ring. I put a wheel in a gutter running at right-angles to the road and bent a wishbone."

By then he had the gorgeous dark-metallic-green BRM, with its V-8 engine revving to 12,000rpm, handling more to his liking. "He had done enough testing to encourage us," said Tony Rudd, "and, as I found out later, he listened intently and stored away everything I told him." Rudd proved he could be a listener too. Before Easter he and chassis engineer John Crosthwaite had adapted the BRM's suspension to Jackie's driving style. This yielded rich dividends.

Not that it was always easy for Rudd to make out what Stewart needed. He had been used to working with Graham Hill, a meticulous record-keeper who knew what he wanted, whether or not it gave the best results, and American Richie Ginther, who was renowned for his car development skills. Jackie, wrote Rudd, "used a different vocabulary. In fact it took me some time to understand what he was driving at. Things improved significantly during one Snetterton test. After trying unsuccessfully to explain what was wrong with the front end, he told me to try it myself, clapping his helmet on my head – so off I went."

Chief engineers renowned for their talking instead of their driving would have been flummoxed, but not Tony Rudd. He had once driven a V-16 BRM at 200mph between the poplars at Albi to see if it was ready for Juan Fangio, so a few laps at Snetterton were small beer. "I soon realised what he meant," Rudd recalled, "but he could not understand why I just sat in the car looking profoundly wise. When he realised I was stuck and could not get out, he had hysterics."

The racing world was agog when novice Stewart scored a Championship point with sixth in his first race for BRM in the South African Grand Prix at East London in January 1965. This was not the expected form at all. Eoin Young reported that "there were mutterings that Stewart would never match his Formula 3 prowess once he climbed into the BRM; they said he ran away with the Formula 3 races only because he had a better car; they said that a season in Formula 1 would show him that motor racing was really a man's game and that he would cool his heels and his ambitions at the tail end of the pro field."

In the spring Jackie shattered these expectations. At the Easter Goodwood meeting he took pole position with the BRM and in the race set equal fastest lap with Jim Clark at 107.4mph before retiring with camshaft niggles; no one has officially lapped Goodwood faster at this time of writing. In May he dismayed the pundits again with his victory over John Surtees's Ferrari V-8 in another non-Championship race, the BRDC International Trophy at Silverstone. Okay, Clark and Gurney were away at Indianapolis and Hill and Brabham had retired, but beating the experienced Surtees was a great achievement for a newcomer to Formula 1.

Surtees didn't dissent. "The Scottish new boy drove very well indeed to hold his first place," he wrote. "I realised that Stewart would have to make an error of judgement if the places were to be reversed. Well, he made no error on that day and, on his performance as I saw it, I thought he had worked well for and had thoroughly deserved his first Formula 1 win."

In 1965 Jackie qualified five times on the front row of Championship grids and finished second three times behind Jim Clark's Lotus, with which he was "completely satisfied," he told Peter Manso. "Sure I wanted to win, but I was satisfied with finishing second because I was so much further ahead of everybody else." He only retired three times, once when he ran out of road at the Nürburgring as mentioned earlier. This was a tribute to the quality of the technical support that BRM gave to its new recruit.

Charmingly, Jackie attributed some of his early success to the fact that the steps on the ladder were not so far apart in those racing years: "I was very lucky in many ways to start racing Formula 1 when I did. The big advantage was that the 1½-litre Formula was still going then, which made the transition from Formula 2 that much easier." He also felt that he had been fortunate to slot into a period in Grand Prix racing when he was the main 'coming man'. Timmy Mayer's death had removed a rival and opened an opportunity for Jackie with Tyrrell. Soon Stewart would be chased by Chris Amon, Mike Spence and Jacky Ickx, but he did have his early years much to himself.

Near the end of the 1965 season Stewart chatted with the delightful Canadian journalist Chris McCall. "Eighteen months ago I was nobody. I've come up very fast through the ranks, and I never really expected to do as well as I have this year," he told her. "As a matter of fact, it's always amazed me when I have won *anything*, because I think everybody is much better than I am. And I'm not trying to sound … well, you know, modest.

"People don't realise how good the fellows that I'm racing with are – Surtees, Clark, Gurney, Graham and the rest. They're all first-rate. Now everybody's watching me. If I don't keep going well, or if I don't win the Championship, they'll say I'm not living up to my promise. A prediction like 'World Champion' makes it all the harder to do anything well."

Arguments raged all winter over the finish of the last European Grand Prix of 1965 at Monza, which the cheeky Stewart stole from under the nose of team-mate and Championship contender Graham Hill to win his first *Grande Epreuve* – a race counting for points. Thanks to an engine tweak the BRMs had the legs of the field and the final laps were a needle match between Stewart and Hill, who were slipstreaming each other to stay ahead of Dan Gurney's Brabham.

"It was difficult for me in this situation," recapped Jackie, "because my car was quicker through the South Turn than Graham's. I was certainly faster out of the turn, and with our slipstreaming it meant that whatever I did on those last few laps I led past the starting line." Hill commented, "As far as I was concerned I was going to win that race." The atmosphere in the pits can be imagined. "We tried everything to slow them down," said Tony Rudd.

Rocketing through the fast South Turn on the last lap but one, Stewart's BRM had the inside line. "I moved over to give him room," said Graham. "We had the race in the bag so there wasn't any sense in chopping up my own team-mate but I wouldn't have moved if it had been anyone else." Stewart looked over to see Hill sawing at the steering to correct a slide: "Graham went wide only to strike the loose stuff that gets to the outside of a corner during a race." Jackie gained a three-second advantage which, in the absence of team orders, he held over the final lap to the chequered flag.

If this victory gave Stewart momentum in the BRM set-up he certainly knew how to use it. He gave enthusiastic support to BRM's entry of two 2-litre racers in the Tasman series of ten 100-mile races in Australia and New Zealand in early 1966. "Jackie completely dominated the Championship," recalled Tony Rudd, "ably supported by Dickie Attwood."

Stewart won the Teretonga Trophy and Lady Wigram races as well as the two Longford races and the Sandown Park event on his way to the Championship. Eoin Young wrote, "Having never seen the twisty 1½-mile Teretonga circuit near Invercargill, Stewart took only seven exploratory laps to better the lap record!"

This was the kind of achievement that provoked author Peter Manso to ask Jackie just why he was such a good racing driver. "I'm damned if I know and I mean that, I really mean it," the Scot replied. "It's not bullshit and it's not evading the question. I don't know. I don't know if it's the way I drive the racing car or whether everybody's slower or something. I honestly don't know. It's a very natural thing for me, driving a racing car. If you do something naturally, you don't know why you're better at that than somebody else."

Racing one of the Tasman BRMs, a full litre down on the three unsupercharged litres allowed by the new Grand Prix Formula 1 for 1966, Jackie opened his new season's account with victory in the Monaco Grand Prix. The young man seemed touched with magic. He had a new BRM contract that "offered me a really good amount" over and above the 1965 figure. "I certainly wanted to stay with them in 1966," he said, with a spectacular new 16-cylinder BRM on the stocks, "and even though things were bad I decided to continue in 1967 because of the great atmosphere within the team."

Jackie couldn't have imagined that his Monaco victory would be his last in Grand Prix racing for two seasons. Not until the Dutch GP in June of 1968 would he wear one of those wonderful Formula 1 laurel wreaths again. For the hottest driver on the Grand Prix circuit the 1966 and 1967 seasons suddenly went stone cold.

The culprit was the new BRM engine, which was composed of two flat-eights geared together. Although it developed 420 horsepower it was rough and unreliable and contributed to a car that weighed a swingeing 250lb more than the Formula 1 minimum. "The car had exceptional road holding," Tony Rudd recalled, "but the problem was it was so dreadfully heavy, which made it sluggish under acceleration."

In his foreword to Tony Rudd's wonderful book, *It was fun! My fifty years of high performance*, Jackie's tongue was only slightly cheekwards when he wrote, "I am not sure that I will ever forgive him for having me drive round in circles with a very clumsy H-16 BRM for more miles than I care to think of; but I suppose I should put it down to character-building."

So cantankerous was the new car that BRM kept racing its Tasman V-8s, enlarged to 2-litres, in the early 1967 season against the 3-litre opposition. Neither car could offer Stewart much in the way of reliability. Of the 19 Grands Prix he entered in those two desolate years, he retired in no fewer than 14. His best finish was second at Spa in 1967, returning to the course where he had crashed so heavily the year before. Jackie, obliged to hold the gear lever in fifth while driving with one hand much of the time, led but had to give best to Dan Gurney and his Eagle-Weslake.

These travails sorely tested an aspect of the Stewart philosophy that he explained to Peter Manso: "If I weren't winning, hadn't a chance of winning, I think then perhaps I would lose a lot of the pleasure because I'm basically a competitive person. You see, in motor racing, I've always been fortunate enough to be involved in winning, in whatever class of racing I've been coming through. I've always been in with a chance." That Jackie was able to maintain this state of mind through these gruesome seasons was a tribute to the tender loving care he received from BRM. Not for nothing was his BRM seat trimmed in Stewart tartan – a genial surprise from Tony Rudd.

In 1967, the year he'd hoped that the H-16 would come good, Jackie saw Graham Hill leave BRM and take up a drive that might have been his own: teaming with Clark at Lotus, whose GP racer was powered from mid-year by the potent and light new Ford-Cosworth DFV V-8. Denny Hulme was World Champion that year but it seemed unlikely that anything would catch the Clark/Lotus/Ford juggernaut in 1968. One team, however, had the means to manage it: Ferrari. And Ferrari, like Jackie, was contracted to the fuels and oils of Shell, which promoted the benefits of an alliance to Ferrari team manager Franco Lini.

With some trepidation, in view of Enzo Ferrari's reputation as a manipulator of drivers, Stewart visited Maranello in June 1967 for initial talks. The great Italian team had a seat to fill: that of the much-missed Lorenzo Bandini, killed at Monte Carlo the month before. Accompanied by Lini, Jackie went to Ferrari "very unwillingly, but I must admit to being very impressed with the place." Among others he met Ferrari's son, Piero Lardi Ferrari. At another meeting in August "we talked finance, in fact it was completely agreed financially, and Ferrari seemed a superb organisation for making racing cars, just what I was looking for. One of the things that attracted me to Ferrari was Mauro Forghieri, for I am sure that I could have worked very well with him because he is such a practical man."

A deal looked set for Jackie to join Chris Amon to form a formidable Ferrari driving team for 1968. But then Stewart sent in his Scottish solicitors to dot the i's and cross the t's, and before he knew it Ferrari had announced the signing of Jacky Ickx to partner Amon, "because Jackie Stewart had asked for too much money." This wasn't so, but presumably the Belgian Ickx seemed more biddable. (Ferrari's antipathy for nit-picking lawyers of the Anglo-Saxon persuasion had already been amply demonstrated in his abortive 1965 negotiations over the possible sale of his company to Ford.)

Preferring drivers to be awed and stunned by the opportunity to race his cars, Enzo Ferrari had not taken to the forthright manner of the Scot, who, according to Franco Lini, objected to being called "*Inglese*" in the discussions. Nevertheless in his memoirs Ferrari wrote with insightful appreciation: "Stewart was a genuine champion, a man who didn't make many concessions to his adversaries. He knew what he wanted then and knows it now. Aside from the exceptional whisky he gives his friends, I should point out that he is a man who takes account of things, including the risks of racing. He is one of the best of all time."

BRM was not yet a lost cause, although Tony Rudd was well aware that Jackie was losing interest. A new car was on the stocks, one that Stewart had initiated. "He talked Sir Alfred [Owen] into building a V-12-engined car in parallel with the H-16s," Rudd recalled, "and, recognising the tremendous amount of work going through Bourne, suggested we sub-contract the design and build of two cars to Len Terry's company." Terry, who designed some of the Lotuses that Jackie had enjoyed driving, had set up on his own account to create Eagles for Dan Gurney.

Here were the makings of a new BRM which might have the potential to be competitive. "Talks with BRM were continuing" in 1967, said Jackie, "because they had decided to make a V-12 and they offered me very good money." In fact BRM would decide to concentrate on the Terry-built V-12s in 1968 with Mike Spence and Pedro Rodriguez in their cockpits, but poor Mike was killed in practice at Indianapolis. BRM was only a distant fifth in manufacturers' points that season so Stewart can be credited with foresight in abandoning the team's new programme, even though it was his.

In 1968 Louis Stanley was becoming more involved in the management of the BRM team. Jackie penned a portrait of Sir Alfred Owen's brother-in-law: "Louis Stanley is an extraordinary man. He has many talents and some failings, not all of which are obvious to him. He writes a very amusing book, takes terrible pictures and can be diplomatic or not depending on the circumstances. Louis is a big man, a daunting character in many ways with an imperious manner and I had always deferentially called him Mr Stanley when he was there, and like everyone else, Big Lou when he was not."

"Jackie's stay at BRM was a tonic," responded Louis Stanley. "He was enormously popular with everyone. As a driver he impressed with the naturalness of his style, which at times was almost flawless. In the rain he was brilliant, he had the ability to retain the peak of physical fitness and he was one of the severest critics of himself. A tiresome habit was a tendency to chatter – he never stopped and at times the broad accent required the services of an interpreter."

An interpreter would certainly have been needed if Jackie had joined Ferrari! Instead, in 1968 he would join an Anglo-French operation headed by Ken Tyrrell that had no track record whatsoever at the highest level of the sport. Jackie would not stop chattering – he never has or should – and in Ken Tyrrell he would more than meet his match.

The daunting Burnenville Corner of the old Spa-Francorchamps circuit is visited by Stewart in a practice session with the gorgeous little Type 56 BRM V-8. In 1965 he is a worthy second to Jim Clark and in 1966, of course, he crashes with the consequences he describes so vividly in Chapter 1. At Monaco in 1966 (overleaf) he scores his second Grande Epreuve *victory for BRM.*

GOOD

12

Jackie's three years with BRM have their ups and downs. At Watkins Glen in 1966 (above, left to right) JYS, BRM major domo Lou Stanley, engineer Tony Rudd and Graham Hill contemplate their fate. The loquacious Stewart has a word for Hill at Silverstone (below) in May 1965.

Stewart exercises his ability to "paint a picture" of the way his 3-litre BRM H-16 is behaving in 1967 at Mosport Park (above) and at Spa (below) where Jean and Lou Stanley are his audience. In the Belgian race he is second to Dan Gurney after leading and in Canada he reaches fourth before retiring with throttle problems.

Still using their 2-litre BRM V-8s in the first 3-litre Formula season, Stewart and Hill have an inter-team encounter at Zandvoort (above and below) in 1966 and finish fourth and second respectively. Bernard Cahier catches Jackie counter-steering at Mexico City in 1965 (facing page) en route to a retirement with clutch trouble. Snapped by Michael Cooper on a wet Nürburgring Karussell in 1966 (overleaf), Jackie is racing to fifth in the German Grand Prix.

Organisation
6

Abounding opportunities for aviating at the bumpy and hilly Nürburgring are not overlooked by photographer Michael Cooper. Stewart is taking off (above) in his BRM V-8 in 1965 and landing (below) in 1966 – no mean feat. In the 1965 race Jackie retires after damaging the front suspension by hitting a concealed drainage canal at the side of the road.

In 1967 Tony Rudd hopes that the weight of his H-16 BRM will keep it on the road but after leaping (above) it lands even harder (below). Stewart reaches third place in the German GP then retires with rear-axle failure. Jackie's BRM is just below the 'Marathon' sign (overleaf) at the start of the 1967 Italian GP, from which engine trouble retires him.

SHELL
MOTOR OIL
BOSCH
Shell

I.T.E.C.
Shell

FERODO
FERODO
FERODO

DUNLOP
LUCAS
LUCAS

With his H-16 BRM Jackie is battling in the 1967 Canadian GP (above) with Amon's Ferrari (20) and the Brabham-Repco of eventual winner Jack Brabham (1) before retiring. Mexico's heat (right) inspires the truncated nose of the H-16 in 1966 but Jackie retires, as he does the same year at Watkins Glen (overleaf) in a frustrating season. At the Glen start captured by Stanley Rosenthall, Bandini (9), winner Clark (1) and Brabham leap ahead; JYS is behind the Cooper-Maserati (7) of John Surtees. At Silverstone in 1967 (page 96) Jackie is reflecting on his options for 1968. Ferrari is among them.

JYS thrusts his 2-litre BRM amongst the 3-litre big boys at the start of the 1966 Belgian GP (opposite top). Though the start is dry, rain is waiting on the other side of the circuit with the consequences shown on page 17. In the 1966 British GP at Brands (opposite bottom) Stewart passes a Hill/Clark duel but is halted by an engine failure.

DUNLOP

Buco

4

The learning years with Britain's BRM bring some good results, such as third at Monaco in 1965 (preceding page) and second behind Dan Gurney in the Belgian Grand Prix in 1967 (facing page), where Jackie has to drive with one hand and hold the gear lever in place with the other. With the weighty H-16 BRM he retires from the 1966 Italian GP at Monza (above) with a fuel leak and misfire and takes the flag in the T-car (below) at the end of practice at Watkins Glen the same year. His engine blows in a big way at half-distance.

SHELL
DUNLOP

Faces of a racer (opposite): Still with a taped-on fabric helmet tartan in his all-conquering Cooper-BMC of 1964 (top left); celebrating his first Formula 1 win in the non-Championship race at Silverstone in May 1965 (top right); in determined mood before the 1967 BOAC 500 at Brands Hatch (bottom left), and happier than he and Ken Tyrrell have any right to be after his first test of the March 701 in February 1970 (bottom right). Jackie and his wife Helen make their own Grand Prix preparations in their own ways.

Although renowned for his Grand Prix exploits, Stewart also excels in other arenas. With Chris Amon in a P4 he places second at Brands Hatch in 1967 (top) to bring Ferrari the points that clinch a Manufacturers' World Championship. He tigers the flighty Lola-Chevy T260 to third in the 1971 Can-Am standings (bottom). And he comes tantalisingly close to victory in the 1966 Indianapolis 500 in a Mecom-entered Lola-Ford (opposite).

4

Max Le Grand captures the gritty mood of Formula 1 racing in the 1960s with his superb portraits: Stewart's BRM at Monaco in 1965 (preceding pages); Jackie's return (left) in his 1969 Matra-Ford to the Nürburgring paddock where (above) he accommodates his youthful fans in the casual style of the era, and Stewart's total focus on the task ahead as he prepares for battle in the 1970 March-Ford (facing page).

DUNLOP
elf
elf
DUNLOP
Ford
Autolite
Autolite

elf
MATRA
elf

DUNLOP
elf
7
FORD
FORD

In 1969 Jackie attacks the tortuous Monte Carlo roads on his way to pole position in the Matra-Ford MS80 (preceding pages). Its rear wing has just been amputated by an FIA diktat. *He retires in the race with failures of faulty U-joints. At the Nürburgring the same year he tests – but decides not to race – the four-wheel-drive MS84 Matra (above) engineered by Derek Gardner, who will design his Tyrrell-Fords.*

A measure of the Stewart margin of superiority in his second Championship year, 1971, is his lead over the Ferraris of Ickx and Regazzoni after the first lap of the German Grand Prix (right). He wins by half a minute ahead of Tyrrell-Ford team-mate François Cévert. Rubens Barrichello (overleaf) brings Stewart Grand Prix its first points and podium with second place in a wet 1997 Monaco GP.

elf
2
Continental

VISIT
MALAYSIA
Havoline
TEXACO
22
Havoline
SANYO
SANYO
HSBC
HSBC

MATRA

FORD
Autolite

CHAPTER 5

Cock of the walk

"What a dump!" A man with a word for every occasion, Ford's Walter Hayes needed only three to sum up his first impression of the premises in which Ken Tyrrell proposed to establish a world-beating Formula 1 team. Hayes was standing under the wooden beams supporting the gabled roof of a barn-like building that Tyrrell had bought for £50 from the Women's Royal Army Corps and plunked down on property flanking his timber yard.

Walter Hayes was the Fleet Street veteran who had taken a robust grip on the public affairs of Ford of Britain and launched the company into motorsport. He was in the wilds of Surrey to check the credentials of one of the many Grand Prix teams that were clamouring to be allowed to use the Ford-sponsored Cosworth DFV racing engine that had shown such chilling potential since its winning launch at Zandvoort in 1967. If Hayes didn't like what he saw at Ockham, Tyrrell wouldn't get engines. And the first impression had not been good.

Is that a hint of a smile we see behind the Stewart balaclava as he pedals his Matra-Ford MS10 toward one of his team's three 1968 victories? He should *smile for Bernard Cahier; the Tyrrell-entered Matra ends a very long dry spell between wins for Jackie. Appropriately enough (preceding page) he wins the Race of Champions at Brands Hatch at the beginning of the 1969 season that brings him the first of his three driver's crowns.*

What, after all, did Tyrrell have to offer Hayes? Like any team manager preparing for a new season, he was juggling all the ingredients – car, driver, engine, sponsors – to try to put together a package that would work. And he had a bigger mountain to climb than most: he had never fielded a Formula 1 entry. Neither had Tyrrell's Formula 2 efforts been touched with glory. In fact after his huge success in Formula 3 with Jackie Stewart in 1964 Ken's minor-formula efforts had stalled.

In 1965 at Reims on 4 July Jackie could finish only fifth in fast Formula 2 company. At the same race meeting a jockey-sized Frenchman named Jean-Pierre Beltoise won the Formula 3 race by inches after a ding-dong battle. The ecstatic Beltoise experienced "a mad happiness. My heart was about to explode." His

Cosworth-prepared Ford engine was routine enough for the category but his chassis was novel: a French-made Matra.

This was the first victory for a Matra car, a racer that had only been designed that spring for a marque that was new the year before. Following as it did a series of failed race entries, the Beltoise victory at Reims came just in time to preserve the future of Matra's racing venture and its cheeky emblem, the head of a speedy fighting cock. Matra chief Jean-Luc Lagardère gave his engineers the green light to carry on and to build more ambitious racing cars: "It was on that day that we decided to go all the way. At Reims we passed the point of no return."

Anglophile French journalist and racing enthusiast Gerard 'Jabby' Crombac was more aware than most of the significance of the Beltoise-Matra victory. He thought his English friends should know what was afoot. At Reims Crombac drew Ken Tyrrell's attention to the success of a new racing chassis, which might possibly interest him one day. In reply Tyrrell was even more economical in his use of words than Walter Hayes: "It's hopeless." The French might make fine wines and fashions, but racing cars? *Jamais*.

Ken Tyrrell had forgotten this incident by the end of the 1965 season when he journeyed to Paris for the awarding of the trophies in the French Formula 2 series. During the ceremonies Jabby Crombac introduced Jean-Luc Lagardère to Tyrrell. Clearly well-briefed by Crombac, the personable and persuasive Lagardère made his case to Tyrrell: his team and his driver should be using a Matra chassis.

"When I first met Lagardère I did not even know there was a car called the Matra," Tyrrell said later. "Lagardère wanted Stewart to test drive a Matra with a Formula 2 BRM engine. I was not interested in the least but Lagardère kept pushing." Over dinner at the posh Tournebroche des Trois Soleils restaurant at Orly Airport, Lagardère made Tyrrell an offer he couldn't refuse: if Ken would loan Matra a BRM engine, Matra would install this and bring the car to Britain for Jackie Stewart to test. Tyrrell agreed.

Ken now had a demanding task. He had to persuade Jackie to step into the cockpit of this unknown car. Stewart: "'What sort of car's this?' 'It's a French car.' Well, this spelt trouble to me immediately. I couldn't imagine why Ken wanted a French car unless as a result of a particularly good evening in Paris and somebody giving him a good line of chat. However he was persistent and told me all about the impressive Matra record in Formula 3. We decided to have a test session."

Tyrrell's four-cylinder BRM engine was installed at Matra's Velizy workshops in a modified Formula 3 chassis which was air-lifted to Gatwick in a Bristol freighter moonlighting from its usual chore of transporting racehorses. There it was met by a Matra truck which transported the test car to Goodwood. "Stewart tried the car," Tyrrell recalled. "He stopped after a few laps to tell me that he had never driven such a great car before; it transmitted power to the wheels better than any single-seater he ever drove."

"I went away feeling enthusiastic about Matra," Jackie said, "and Ken prepared to make some sort of arrangement with them for Formula 2 in 1966." The arrangement was that Ken would run two MS5 Matras for Stewart and Ickx, Matra Sport would run two, and a chassis would be sold to John Coombs for Graham Hill – much to the displeasure of Tyrrell and Stewart. Fortunately Hill preferred Coombs's Brabham.

These carefully-crafted applecarts were overturned by the sly Jack Brabham, who negotiated exclusive use of a killer Honda engine for himself and Denny Hulme for 1966, the last year of the one-litre Formula 2. Teams running other engines were shut out. "The season *could* have been more successful," reflected Stewart, who was still prepared to think positively about Matra. "I felt the car was competitive but then I had my accident in Belgium and that kept me out of several races."

In 1967, while staying with BRM for a disappointing third season in Formula 1, Stewart was developing his Formula 2 links with Tyrrell and Matra as a prelude to Formula 1 the following season.

For the new 1,600cc Formula 2, Cosworth produced its FVA engine. To suit this Matra built its MS7 with enlarged fuel capacity and improvements based on the detailed feedback its engineers received from Tyrrell and Stewart. At the same time Jackie was lighting fires under the battlements of Ford Dunlop, warning the tyre company's directors and engineers that Goodyear and Firestone were fast making up ground with their racing tyres. Dunlop responded during 1967 with its 970 compound, which did the trick.

Stewart, Tyrrell and Matra scored their first joint victories on two successive weekends in August 1967, thousands of kilometres apart: the first at Karlskoga in Sweden and the second after two heats at Pergusa in Sicily. The third and fourth Formula 2 victories came the following month at Jackie's old Cheshire stamping grounds, Oulton Park, and at Albi's historic road circuit in France. Stewart sat on the pole in both and set fastest lap as well, signalling his attainment of the sovereignty that was to become his hallmark.

These successes against strong opposition came at a crucial time for Jackie Stewart. Between the Swedish and Sicilian races he had paid his second visit to Maranello to talk terms with Ferrari. When Ferrari offered the 1968 drive to Jacky Ickx, this gave Ken Tyrrell a ghost of a chance to inveigle Stewart into his own team at the sport's top level. "My only worry," he said, "was whether Jackie thought we were a good enough team for him to drive for in Formula 1."

In spite of Tyrrell's primitive accommodation he had a promise of Cosworth engines from Ford. The latter's Stuart Turner recalled Tyrrell's approach to Jackie to drive in Formula 1 for him:

"Jackie swiftly said: 'You can't afford me.'

"Ken parried with: 'How much?'

"Equally speedily JYS retorted: '£20,000.'

"'It's a deal,' quoth Mr Tyrrell, still wondering where he could get the money."

"I did not see that he had any hope at all of putting the deal together," Jackie mused, "because he needed money and he needed all sorts of other things." Some of the funding came from Dunlop, which wanted to concentrate its Formula 1 efforts on Tyrrell and Stewart. Some came from Ford. And by the time of the Italian Grand Prix at Monza in the second week of September, when Jackie finally said *addio* to Ferrari, Tyrrell had assembled most of the pieces of his puzzle.

Meanwhile Matra had launched its own Formula 1 programme, backed by a loan from the French Government that was only refundable in case of success. This allowed Matra to lay down its own V-12 engine and design a completely new car to carry it, the MS11. But Jean-Luc Lagardère realised that this would be a winning car no sooner than 1969; there was 1968 to deal with in the meantime. This time it was Ken Tyrrell who had to turn on the charm. Pointing to the results achieved in Formula 2, he asked Matra to supply a chassis to which he could bolt his Ford-Cosworth engines.

An ingenious solution was engineered, one that would ensure energetic flying of the Matra flag in 1968 and also bring a Cosworth-powered car into the family to act as a yardstick for the progress of Matra's own V-12. A new team was created, Matra International, subsuming Tyrrell's operation with the backing of the big new French national petroleum company, Elf. It would use chassis on loan from Matra and would supply its own engines. Dunlop tyres would be worn both by Matra International and the works team, Matra Sport. The Tyrrell-run team would concentrate on the health and welfare of just one driver: John Young Stewart. Ken Tyrrell had pulled it off.

"I liked Ken and had confidence in his management," Jackie reflected on the deal. "It seemed the logical thing to do at the time; looking back I suppose it was quite courageous of all of us to undertake the Matra project. The engine had been proved, the chassis seemed competitive, and so, I felt, was I. The team manager and the mechanics were good and we had all worked together before. Yet it was done with a feeling of hope rather than an expectation of winning the World Championship."

Others equally knowledgeable saw more than a minor threat in the newly-formed Franco-Britannic *équipe*. Assessing the opposition for 1968 Jack Brabham put Lotus, Ferrari and Gurney's Eagle at the top of his list and added, "Then there would be Tyrrell with Jackie Stewart in a Matra-Ford – that sounded like an ideal set-up for going racing. We felt they might upset quite a lot of their rivals' plans."

Upset them they might, but the hastily-assembled new team had precious little time to make preparations before the first *Grande Epreuve* of 1968 on New Year's Day at the high altitude of Kyalami in South Africa. Matra chassis designer Bernard Boyer made ready a lashed-up test car that could be used for initial trials of the chassis and tyres. It was adapted from a Formula 2 monocoque with uprated suspension, wheels and brakes and powered by one of Tyrrell's Cosworth V-8s.

Jackie first set foot in the MS9 for brief trials at Velizy on 12 December followed by some laps at lunchtime on a damp Montlhéry road circuit the following day before the crude test car was airlifted to Kyalami, which Tyrrell had booked long ago for Dunlop tyre tests. (With stunning symmetry another Anglo-French engineering collaboration, the supersonic Concorde airliner, was rolled out at Toulouse on 11 December.)

Painted only in sick-green primer, festooned with pipes and provisional gubbins, the Matra MS9 "looked like something you would use on a farm," said its driver. Truth to tell, a glossy finish was always secondary for Matra; the Formula 2 cars were called "tatty" by the press when they turned up at the beginning of 1967. But the MS9 inspired the question, "Would you send the kid out in a crate like that?"

Ken Tyrrell entered two Formula 2 Matras for the South African Grand Prix for Stewart and Beltoise, ballasted up to the Formula 1 minimum weight. He also requested an entry for the MS9 – just in case. To the amazement of the Matra executives and engineers, he took up the option.

Phenomenally, the 'bitza' from Velizy was third fastest in qualifying. From the three-car front row Stewart exploited its excellent traction to rocket into a lead which he held for the first lap before being caught up by Clark's Lotus-Ford. Clark's team-mate Graham Hill also got by but no one else threatened Jackie until his Cosworth threw a connecting rod just past half-distance. "We knew we were competitive," said Stewart with commendable understatement.

Any doubt was eradicated by a test session at Kyalami after the race. Roger Hill and Max Rutherford bolted on a fresh DFV so Jackie and Dunlop could get down to serious tyre testing – a science Tyrrell and Stewart are credited with originating. Over ten days the 'mule' travelled 1,361 miles at racing speeds. Of the 534 laps Jackie turned, 156 were quicker than the new lap record Jim Clark had just set in the race.

A huge gap yawned in the Formula 1 calendar before the next race in Spain on 12 May. By mid-March, in time for the Race of Champions at Brands Hatch, the Matra boffins had completed their proper Formula 1 car for Tyrrell, the MS10. Although Jackie threw it around the circuit to qualify third fastest, the high unsprung weight of its provisional suspension parts made the new Matra-Ford a handful at bumpy Brands. After a pit stop to sort out tangled pedal pads he finished sixth.

If this were not discouraging enough, the McLaren team turned up with neat new orange cars also powered by the Cosworth DFV. And Jackie's qualifying time was bettered by Mike Spence in the new Terry-built BRM with its V-12 engine – the very package that Stewart had initiated during the previous season, his last with BRM. The new BRM looked good, Pedro Rodriguez's finishing second in the race behind Bruce McLaren. Jackie could be excused for wondering if he'd made the right move.

The events of April 1968 threw Stewart's well-planned life into disarray. To safeguard his increasingly high earnings, subject to 93 percent tax by Britain's Labour government, he emigrated to Switzerland to become a tax exile. This obliged him to remain outside Britain for some time to establish his overseas residency. But only four days after his move to Geneva came the stunning news of the death of Jim Clark on the fifth lap of the first heat of a wet Formula 2 race at Hockenheim on 7 April. Stewart was granted special dispensation by the Prime Minister's office to attend the funeral in Scotland of his countryman, friend, mentor and indeed idol.

At the end of April Jackie was back at Jarama in Spain, where he'd been when he heard of Clark's crash, to race a Formula 2 Matra-Ford. For the 1968 season John Coombs's team was preparing and entering the still-successful MS7 Formula 2 cars under the Matra International banner and Ken Tyrrell's direction. Stewart had already won two races in the minor formula in the new season and looked set fair to add another when, at the end of a practice session, he locked a wheel on braking and slid into a fencepost with his hands well cranked over on the steering wheel. The kickback, the doctors told him later, caused a painful hairline fracture in a bone in his right wrist. Instead of racing at Jarama he became the event's honorary starter.

Thus began a frustrating month and then some for John Young Stewart, who missed a potentially lucrative Indy 500 and points-earning Formula 1 races at Jarama and Monte Carlo in which Matras showed excellent pace. Jackie's right forearm was in plaster, on his doctor's advice, but for the Belgian Grand Prix at Spa on 9 June he felt ready to have a go. He had a special plastic casing made that could be laced around his wrist to stiffen it enough so he could shift and brace the wheel.

This brave effort almost paid off. Jackie was second-fastest qualifier next to Chris Amon's Ferrari and after the start, shifting with difficulty and helped by retirements, he made his way into the lead. But as he approached the beginning of his last lap he detected fuel starvation and had to dart into his pit for a splash of petrol – after which a flat battery wouldn't start the engine. In fact four gallons remained but the fuel system failed to pick them up. Jackie was credited with fourth place.

Out of the plaster and into the plastic splint again for Zandvoort two weeks later, Jackie's wrist injury was aggravated on the twisty Dutch track by the MS10's dithering under braking and an excess of understeer. But he received a gift on race day: rain. "When the race started," Graham Hill recalled, "it was pouring with rain and I was having a bit of a thrash when Stewart went by as if I had been tied to a post. He just disappeared in a cloud of spray and I never saw him again until he lapped me – very unfair."

Reduced traction on the wet tarmac eased the strain on his wrist and with the help of Dunlop's latest compound Stewart was able to give Matra its first Formula 1 victory at Zandvoort. "There is no question," he said, "that had it been dry I could not have completed the distance, never mind win." With Beltoise's Matra V-12 placing second, the French newspapers were less restrained. "The Day of Glory Has Arrived," they headlined.

Ironically, in mid-season aerospace firm Matra was less quick than other Grand Prix car builders to cotton on to the fitting of wings to generate downforce, which ranked with wider wheels and tyres as the big innovation of 1968. Its progress was hampered by the strikes of May and June that blocked supplies and halted work in France; strikers welded shut the hangar doors of Matra's Velizy neighbour, Dassault. But Matra quickly made up lost ground and initiated work on a completely new car for 1969, the MS80.

In and out of plaster and plastic on his right wrist, Stewart managed third in the French GP at Rouen and sixth in the British race at Brands Hatch after a struggle with the car and track that gave Jackie "more pain in this race than any other I have ever taken part in." Still, in a spotty season he was in with a chance for the Championship. Jackie closed on Graham Hill's points lead with a sensational victory at the Nürburgring, a race he ranks among his very best.

Mist and heavy rain loomed all weekend above the sinuous 14.2-mile track through the Eifel Mountains. At the start, said Jackie, "the spray was absolutely unbelievable – I couldn't see anything at all! I couldn't see my braking distance marks; I couldn't see the car in front; it was just a great wall of spray." He dismissed this difficulty by driving into a first-lap lead that he extended to a winning margin of a stunning four minutes over the rest of the field. He had time to climb out of his car to join Tyrrell to see who would be coming through in second place! "It was a tremendously satisfying race to win," Jackie related, "but I was very pleased to get it over with."

Two weeks later Jackie defeated a strong field in the non-Championship Oulton Park Gold Cup and in October he led from first lap to last at Watkins Glen to take the American Grand Prix. Placing only seventh in Mexico after sundry mechanical problems, Stewart had to settle for second in the 1968 World Championship, with 36 points to Hill's 48.

Next year it all came good for the Stewart-Tyrrell-Matra-Ford-Cosworth-Elf-Dunlop combination. "We decided to start early for 1969," said Jackie, "and this more than anything else was responsible for the 1969 success." Of the 2,323 Grand Prix miles raced that year, Stewart led 1,167 – just over half. "Jackie drove brilliantly," acknowledged Graham Hill. "The cars themselves were beautifully prepared – this was largely because they did a great deal of testing – and they thoroughly deserved their success."

In the first eight races of 1969 the finishing list was topped by Jackie Stewart with two exceptions: Monaco, with retirement after virtually-simultaneous universal-joint failures for Stewart and team-mate Beltoise, and second place at the Nürburgring after a tough struggle with Jacky Ickx's Brabham-Ford.

Jackie clinched the World Championship with his final victory of the season at Monza. He dramatically outfumbled Rindt, Beltoise and McLaren on the last corner of the last lap to win a race in which less than a fifth of a second covered the top four finishers. A triumphant year for Stewart ended with fourth place in the Mexican Grand Prix and, helped by Jean-Pierre Beltoise's placings, with the Manufacturers' Championship as well for Matra.

Was this a lively springboard for success next year? Not at all, as it happened. For 1970 Matra, which had new commercial arrangements with Simca instead of Ford, wanted to field its own all-French team with new V-12 engines. Jackie was invited to drive one, and in back-to-back tests at Albi he equalled his time in the MS9-Ford with a modified MS11-Matra V-12. He preferred a Ford-powered car, however, and Matra would no longer provide chassis to Tyrrell. Tyrrell and Stewart had it all to do over again.

If the spectators captured by Michael Cooper are not looking at the sparkling front row of Amon (Ferrari), Stewart (Matra) and Hill (Lotus) on this sunny August day at Oulton Park in 1968 it is because the start for the 110-mile Gold Cup is being flagged by none other than five times World Champion Juan Manuel Fangio. Stewart leads throughout ahead of Chris Amon; they share fastest lap.

GOLD LEAF
TEAM LOTUS
2

In the months when he is troubled by a fractured bone in his right wrist, rain lightens the steering load enough to ease Jackie's task at two crucial 1968 races that bring welcome wins at Zandvoort in June (above) and at a sodden Nürburgring in August (left). Dunlop helps as well with a tyre compound and tread design that copes with these conditions.

Bernard Cahier braves the elements to capture Stewart's drive to victory (right, above) and the podium (right) at the Nürburgring shared with second-place Graham Hill, right, and third-place Jochen Rindt on the left. In sunnier conditions with a healthy wrist Jackie presses hard at the Oulton Gold Cup in 1968, locking a front wheel on his way to victory (overleaf).

Gulf
Firestone

DUNLOP
FORD
5

elf
MATRA
Ford

Late 1968 and early 1969 see an explosion of high-mounted wings on Formula 1 cars that is ended by the sporting authorities at the 1969 Monaco GP. Jackie leads from the start (above) to win the Brands Hatch Race of Champions in March 1969. Stewart calls Barcelona's Montjuich (below and right, bottom) "a 'graunchy' circuit that does not need driving ability so much as concentration and hard work, rather like Monte Carlo." Stewart starts from the second row and wins, avoiding the crashes caused by failed wings that lead to the ban at Monaco. In 1968 pole-sitter Mario Andretti gets the drop on Jackie at the start of the US Grand Prix at Watkins Glen (top right) but Stewart catches him before the lap is over and leads to the finish.

Many faces of Matra. The first appearance of the MS10-Ford at Brand Hatch in March of 1968 in the Race of Champions (top) only hints at its future form, Stewart finishing sixth. At Monte Carlo in 1969 (centre and opposite) the new MS80 shows off the superb workmanship of its hull, crafted by an artisan who built prototype aircraft for Morane-Saulnier. This is also stunningly portrayed in the MS80 depicted at Barcelona's Montjuich (overleaf). In the US Grand Prix (bottom) Jackie is already 1969 World Champion when he retires with engine failure.

E
DUNL
Autolite
7

7
MATRA
Ford
elf

Stewart's Matra-Ford MS80 during practice (this page and facing page bottom) for the French GP in July 1969 at the five-mile Charade circuit near the tyre-making city of Clermont-Ferrand, which he called "probably one of the four most difficult tracks in the world. There are two very similar places on the circuit, two corners where the scenery is alike and you have to think out every lap which one you are approaching."

"You have to go easy during the first few laps at Clermont because it is very important on such a circuit to see signs of any oil trace in good time," Jackie adds. "It is difficult with the blind corners and hills, and the parts of the road shaded by trees, to see oil which may have been left by the other cars on the first lap." With dark visor in place (above) he avoids all hazards to run away with the 1969 race.

Two Matra-Ford seasons of 1968 and 1969 prove the merit of teamwork between epic arguers for their respective points of view, Jackie Stewart and Ken Tyrrell. Their attention is directed elsewhere (left) and Ken lends his ears to Jackie (above). Former Tyrrell team-mate Jacky Ickx wins the 1969 German GP (below) but Stewart isn't unhappy with second after a rousing duel with Ickx. Bruce McLaren is a satisfied third. At Silverstone in 1969's British GP Jochen Rindt keeps Jackie honest (overleaf) but the Scot prevails, driving his team-mate's car after his own is damaged in a practice crash.

ELF

ELF
3

15
Autolite

15
elf
Autolite

15
elf
15

For the penultimate Grande Epreuve *of 1968 in October at Watkins Glen the Matra-Ford MS10 is a cleaned-up piece of kit with its smoother cockpit surround and neatly-braced rear wing. Stewart circulates among the Armco barriers he did so much to encourage, brakes hard for the turn before the pits and takes the chequered flag from an aviating Tex Hopkins after leading all 108 laps to win at an average speed of 124.89mph.*

CHAPTER 6

Scottish ambassador

Kitted out in kilts and sporrans, the Stewart youngsters had flaunted distinctive tartans to confirm their individuality: Hunting Stewart for Jimmy and Royal Stewart for Jackie. So when Helen McGregor, soon to be Helen Stewart, had the inspiration of pinning a strip of tartan around Jackie's helmet for a race at Charterhall her choice was naturally Royal Stewart. Later painted on, the distinctive tartan band became the bold trademark of J. Y. Stewart the racing driver.

Jackie was one of the first drivers to flaunt such a personalised presentation. Manfred von Brauchitsch favoured a red cloth helmet, Tazio Nuvolari a yellow jersey, Mike Hawthorn a dark-blue crash hat with a white visor, not unlike Jim Clark later, and Dan Gurney a menacing black helmet. But the concept of an identifying pattern in Jackie's era was matched only by Graham Hill's London Rowing Club stripes.

Bernard Cahier's portrait of Jackie Stewart exceeds the usual thousand-word quotient for a picture with its look of resigned and introspective intelligence. Few men have been better equipped to cope with all the aspects of a career as a professional racing driver.

With his buccaneering looks, distinctive helmet and wry humour, Graham Hill was one of the boldest personalities of the Grand Prix world in the late 1950s and early 1960s, a time of transition from the era when the car was all-important in Formula 1 racing. Great marques like Mercedes-Benz, Maserati, Ferrari, Alfa Romeo and Lancia competed; they built and raced their cars themselves using the most advanced technology of the era. Theirs were the laurels and the glory and their drivers were secondary.

First with Coventry Climax engines and later with the ubiquitous Ford-Cosworth V-8, Formula 1 cars gained a measure of equality of performance during the 1960s. As a result the Drivers' World Championship, established in 1950, loomed larger in importance. By the early 1970s this was the championship that counted. With the noble exception of Ferrari, racing cars no longer bore the names of the great car manufacturers. No one much minded if the car was a March, Tyrrell, McLaren or Brabham, none of them household names; the driver became all-important.

In this new racing era, in the wake of Graham Hill and Jim Clark, Jackie Stewart was the first great protagonist. With his World Championships in 1969, 1971 and 1973 he stamped his authority on this new driver-centred age, one in which the oft-heard sobriquet 'Ford Formula' accurately described both the fact that most cars used the Ford Cosworth engine and that racing was intensely competitive. Any driver who could assert his dominance of the sport under those conditions had to be good. Jackie Stewart certainly was.

That he used a Scots tartan as his badge of battle was not happenstance. Jackie is a born-and-bred Scot and proud of it. "I was always conscious in all my races that I was racing as a Scotsman, racing for Scotland," he told author Hunter Davies. "Scots are canny, they don't rush in. They digest the whole position and don't act impetuously. They don't take risks and seldom gamble. At the same time, they're very determined, very stubborn, never give up. Those are all good attributes for a racing driver." And for a businessman, he might have added.

His countrymen can also suffer from a certain sense of inferiority, Jackie said: "Basically, I think Scots are pessimists. They never say, 'I'm going to win that.' I always thought the opposition was superior to me. I had a fear of the opposition, not a fear of death. Perhaps the Scots do have an inferiority complex, whatever they say about being better than the English."

Stewart expressed the same sentiments to Peter Manso: "In sport, in all the things I've done, in my shooting for instance, where I was almost as successful as I've been in motor racing, I never really thought I would ever win anything. I was always pleasantly surprised when I won because I never actually thought that I could beat the other bloke called Rossini who happened to be the World Champion. But when I did beat him, it was a pleasure and surprise. This is almost a Scottish trait, really."

Racing driver John Whitmore extended the courtesy of his flat in London's Balfour Place to both Jim Clark and Jackie Stewart. "We called it the Scottish Embassy," Stewart recalled. "It meant I didn't have to get to know London on my own as an outsider. Jim Clark was then the Champion Formula 1 driver and I was coming up in Formula 3. It was only a two-bedroom apartment, but John also had his country house, and we'd always stay there when we were racing at Brands Hatch."

Jackie Stewart had never been at a loss to present himself effectively. Said a friend from his early racing days, "He always managed to project a standing a bit higher than he was." But the guidance of Clark and Whitmore was valuable to a newcomer who was eager to 'get the clues' of his new environment. "I felt I had bits of haggis and twigs of heather growing out of my ears," Jackie admitted to Hunter Davies. "All the people I met at the English motor clubs seemed so sophisticated in every way. I *had* to win to prove I was as good as them. I loved winning English pound notes and taking them back to Scotland."

Jim Clark and Jackie Stewart had a friendship rooted in their Scottish origins and their common profession but they were rivals on the track. "My admiration for Jimmy was exclusive to my relationship with him," Jackie told Hugh McIlvanney, "because I thought his talent was so fantastic. He was the best racing driver I ever raced against, and I think one of the best drivers in the world. He was that clean, calculating driver, he worked traffic, he saved the car. Jimmy and I drove in very much the same way, smoothly and cleanly and with economy. With us there were no elbows and arms flailing around in the wind. We were precise and unspectacular – rather conservative, in fact."

Stewart interpreted what seems an anomaly to many people: "You've got to be a fairly conservative individual to control your emotions sufficiently to drive a racing car competitively and successfully." Here too his Scots background has a role to play, he explained to McIlvanney: "As a race we are extremely determined, but we are also canny. Ours is not a blind determination. We are very much aware of what is going on. We are able to direct the resolution in our natures into the right channels – to make it effective."

Jackie was starkly realistic about the professional life to which he committed himself for a half-score of his four score and ten years: "You know," he said to Peter Manso, "I think sometimes it's a bloody stupid sport. I get so much pleasure out of doing it personally, and yet sometimes when things go wrong, I really do think it's stupid. You accept that motor racing is totally futile and stupid and still you carry on.

"You are able to do it because what is out there is so exhilarating for the selfish man behind the wheel. When you go back out in the race car you are so totally consumed, the lights go out. You bring your visor down, and it's rose-coloured glasses for whatever time you're out there. It is as if someone has given you an injection that anaesthetises you against the terrible possibilities and leaves you hooked on the marvellous, irreplaceable excitement."

A certain amount of selfishness comes with the territory, Jackie explained to Eoin Young: "You have to have a pretty hard streak in you to win in this business consistently. You've got to be fairly ruthless. You've got to be hard-nosed. That doesn't mean to say that you should not have some sympathy in you, that you can't be a nice person. But you've got to be able to focus your attention when the moment is right, selfishly, in the bullseye of your interest. And everything else must sit second. Whether it's your family, whether it's your loved ones, whether it's other business, whether it's other people, whether it's fans, whether it's sponsors, whether it's mechanics or team owners."

Jackie's ability to distance himself when he judged it necessary won him few friends in the world of motorsports, especially among the press. In the early years he was open with racing scribes, sometimes to excess. As early as 1965, reported Chris McCall, "He reels off his life story in a matter of minutes, complete with catch phrases, for members of the press. Often his glib manner leads people to the conclusion that he's a lightweight. One interviewer remarked after a session with him, 'You know, underneath all that tinsel, I suspect there's just more tinsel.' He was wrong. Stewart's as shrewd as he is pleasant. Being cheery and saying all the right things are part of his job. A major part."

"If I went out there and said all the wrong things," Jackie said to McCall, "opinion would come crashing down on me like a ton of bricks. People would say I'm already getting big-headed. You don't go around being nasty to people. That's the fastest way to lose a ride." Yet in spite of his intentions to the contrary, "big-headed" is just what a lot of people thought of Jackie. He seemed so outwardly comfortable with his early, easy success on the track and so opinionated on so many topics that people assumed his ego was the size of Scotland.

Fellow Scot Eric Dymock warned against such an assumption: "Jackie Stewart's strength lies partly in the self-assurance which he has always possessed. The confident nature and the jaunty, flamboyant, often controversial way Jackie conducts his affairs could give the wrong impression. Someone meeting him for the first time could easily mistake this for conceit but it is not the same thing. He is confident of his ability – he has reason to be. Yet he is too intelligent to get big-headed about it. He is so self-analytical that if he were getting big-headed he would notice it himself."

It was natural enough for Stewart gradually to distance himself from the lower levels of the sport at which he began his career. When his successes brought him in contact with the topmost people at Shell, Elf, Dunlop, Goodyear, Ford and other enterprises he would have been short-sighted not to have nurtured those new relationships with an eye to his future. But to his credit his focus was on the person, not on the position held, for Jackie admires competence, commitment and determination in his colleagues.

"I recognise that there's only so much you can do in your life," Jackie told Russell Bulgin. "I think that there are so many idealists around that all they do is talk and very little action prevails. My belief is that unless you can substantially affect a major happening, then you should not waste time by spinning your wheels."

One of Jackie's rivals on the track, John Surtees, admitted to Graham Gauld that he was in the dreamer category: "Because of our enthusiasm, we put together pictures thinking everybody else is just as enthusiastic as you are, then the practicalities come along. This is the difference between someone like me and, say, Jackie Stewart. He isn't a dreamer, he is just a plain, practical calculating person."

This Stewart frame of mind has had several consequences. One has been a reluctance to delegate. "My experience of people is that you cannot rely on anyone," he said to Eoin Young. "I live my life on the basis of belt-and-braces: that's the way I drove and that's the way I live today." When Stewart was racing he kept complete kits of suits and helmets in a number of key locations so he could always be confident that he had one to hand when needed.

Another consequence is that Jackie is very demanding of those whom he judges competent to share his world. "Weakness really annoys me," he told Peter Manso. "People must be competent about their job. This is one of the things I mean when I say I'm difficult to live with because perhaps I'm more demanding than most people. Just demanding, let's say, of my wife, of how she conducts herself. The same applies to people in business: they've got the basic capabilities perhaps and they don't use them. This annoys me."

A watershed in Jackie Stewart's relations with the press was his decision in 1969, in the midst of the year that was to bring him his first World Championship, to assign his business representation to Mark McCormack's International Management Group. Five years earlier Jackie had considered a similar arrangement as Eoin Young ruefully recalled: "He offered me a job as his manager for a percentage of his earnings. I forget the percentage but he still reminds me that I turned him down – and why not? I was a director of McLaren Racing then and earning £32 a week. Why would I go and do something daft like working for a Scottish Formula 3 driver?"

Mark McCormack was in an altogether different league. Starting with golfer Arnold Palmer, he added Jack Nicklaus to his management stable and later skier Jean Claude Killy and tennis champion Rod Laver, none of whom was or would ever be closely acquainted with poverty row. Stewart was McCormack's first signing in motor racing, a sports arena that looked likely to burgeon in value in the 1970s.

Jackie's previously-easy relationships with members of the press now came under the scrutiny of McCormack's minders, Bud Stanner in the Americas and Jay Michaels in Europe. Photographer Max Le Grand had been accustomed to a relaxed relationship with Stewart, but when he asked if he could hitch a ride with Jackie when he was about to do a couple of Nürburgring laps in a passenger car, Jay Michaels was quickly on the scene – with a request for a $4,000 fee for the experience. "Thereafter we had to meet in obscure places to talk," Le Grand recalled.

Max wasn't the only journalist to feel badly miffed by Jackie's grand new arrangements. Wrote Mary Schnall Heglar before Stewart won his third world crown, "In many ways Jackie has become somewhat removed from his previous contacts, rather like a military officer promoted to HQ. Just between titles his fees have skyrocketed – quintupled in some cases. He *loves* money, and with cheerful rue admits to being a bit hung up on possessing it." If Jackie's press clippings began to be a bit less adulatory after the summer of 1969, and they did, his McCormack deal was at least partly responsible.

One reason the press found it harder to get time with Stewart was that he took on a formidable workload to satisfy both his team and his sponsors. "The number of appearances I did were colossal," he told David Tremayne. "At that time literally every day I was doing something. And I was doing six or eight countries a week, sometimes five or six countries a day. I was making the money I was making because of that.

And I was testing much more than is ever done today. We would go to Kyalami and do two Grands Prix a day for something like 18 days. In those days there really was a tyre war, and no restriction on testing."

Not that Stewart is constitutionally the sort to prefer a quiet life by the home and hearth. Stewart's former boss at BRM, Louis Stanley, was agog at his peripatetic ways: "Jackie's travel itinerary is so time-absorbing that it is difficult to see how anything like a normal home life is possible. He complains, but at the same time he enjoys the role. The endless travel schedule reminds me of *Under Milk Wood*, a play that encapsulates the tumult of living. Its burden is compressed into the remark of Polly Garter, the town tart: 'Isn't life a terrible thing, thank God.' That about sums up Jackie's litany."

Just such a complaint was made to Hunter Davies by Jackie after his retirement from the track in 1973: "I'm still looking for something, a new passion in life. I don't have to set the heather on fire, not this time. I'd want to succeed, naturally, being a competitive person, but not necessarily to win. I know now there are deeper satisfactions than winning. What I want is something to *consume* me. Strangely enough, my first sport, clay pigeon shooting, consumed me more than motor racing. By comparison, that came easy. But where am I going to find a new all-consuming passion?"

Betwixt and between his commitments to Ford, Goodyear, ABC Television, Rolex, Beretta and his shooting school at Gleneagles, Jackie continued to flirt with motorsports. In 1977 he tried the new generation of Formula 1 cars at Paul Ricard and in 1978 he literally crashed a party of veteran drivers racing Ford Escorts at Macao when he inverted his camera car during practice in what he called "one of the worst bloody shunts in my career."

The flirtation turned serious in 1988 when Jackie and his elder son Paul, just turned 21, set up Paul Stewart Racing, or PSR. Their modest initial aim, to enter Paul in Formula Ford, escalated until by 1993 Paul had raced for three years in Formula 3000, the stepping stone to Formula 1 for many drivers. What's more, PSR committed itself to entries in a series of formulae, from Formula Ford to Vauxhall Lotus, through Formula 3 to F3000, creating a 'staircase of talent' that could carry a driver to the top if he had the ability.

After nine years in business PSR could point to a remarkable 107 race victories and ten championships. This was a tribute to the management skills of Paul Stewart, who had relinquished the cockpit after 1993. It could point as well to the successes of several drivers who climbed the PSR staircase. Fellow Scots David Coulthard and Dario Franchitti are among them, as are top-ranked racers Shinji Nakano, Gil de Ferran and Helio Castro-Neves.

However, PSR was far from an 'all-consuming passion' for Paul's dad. Jackie had maintained his strong links with Ford, under a contract that committed his services to them for 125 days a year. Many of these days were spent in test-driving prototype production cars and 'painting pictures' for Ford's engineers just as he did in his racing days. "Most of my work is in testing and developing new cars: chassis, ride and handling," Jackie said. "That's what I enjoy doing most – that's what I do best, in fact. Working with different engineers, hearing different ideas and having different problems to solve ... terrific."

Stewart also showed he was still a speed king when a Benetton-Ford Formula 1 car was brought to Ford's Dearborn ride and handling roads for a series of tests: the competitive Scot posted faster times in the car than both Thierry Boutsen and Alessandro Nannini. "I did know the circuit better than they did," said Jackie in mild mitigation.

Stewart's close ties with the senior executives at Ford often made the difference in the success of new-car programmes. When Jackie felt the Mondeo Contour project was off the rails he didn't hesitate to go over the heads of the engineers and direct to Dearborn with his concerns; we have better Mondeos as a result. And neither did Jackie hesitate when, during a flight in a Ford executive airliner, the talk turned to Ford's distinctly-mediocre profile in Formula 1. Ford needed to make more of a commitment, and over the long term, stressed Stewart. But, asked the Ford chiefs, with whom? Here Jackie had an answer too.

He and Paul prepared that answer carefully. They were not without ideas on the subject. As Paul said, "We'd been round the world exploring various things." They combined all their best notions in a detailed presentation. Paul: "This was the most important proposal we had ever made. We created our proposal to Ford with the help of J. Walter Thompson in Detroit. It was a very elaborate proposal indeed – not something we could have dreamt up overnight, if you like."

On 4 January 1996, in the starry atmosphere of Detroit's International Automobile Show, a £100-million five-year Ford Formula 1 pact with newly-formed Stewart Grand Prix was announced. Here, at last, was the promise of a new all-consuming passion for John Young Stewart.

Uncharacteristically for Stewart, as John Surtees would have pointed out, this was a dream project indeed. But Jackie acknowledged that he was taking a risk. "Anyone can have a dream. The trick is to make it reality. We are still dreaming," he said soon after the project's launch. "We have not delivered yet. There is no racing car. There is no starting grid. There is no podium. We must realise that we will have to learn to crawl and walk before we learn to run."

By 10 December 1996 there was a racing car, and soon after that the SF-1 with its Ford-Cosworth Zetec-R V-10 engine ran for the first time, fittingly at Ford's Boreham test track in Essex. While Paul managed its creation Jackie, chairman of SGP, was tasked with finding the additional tens of millions needed to fund a modern Grand Prix team. It was, he said, the toughest job he'd ever taken on, much more difficult than he'd ever imagined. In one week on the road he visited 13 countries in search of sponsors.

Stewart's success was measured in the commitments he received from Texaco, bankers HSBC, Sanyo and tyremaker Bridgestone, to mention only his most prominent supporters. A new Grand Prix team had been created, one which proudly wore a Stewart tartan, neither Royal nor Hunting but a new design, Racing Stewart, originated in 1995 and registered with The Scottish Tartan Society. And just to keep things in the family, Paul's younger brother Mark was the kingpin of Mark Stewart Productions, the film and video company that followed the fortunes of Stewart Grand Prix.

Closeness to his family is important to Jackie. After he retired from racing he told Peter Manso that "I want to live the family part of my life very fully now. I've been on the road for so long that my family is now one of the major commodities in my life and I don't want to miss any more of the home life with Helen and the boys."

To make good on this commitment while following the fortunes of SGP, Jackie moved his operations base from Clayton House in Switzerland to a four-bedroom flat overlooking the championship golf course at Sunningdale near Ascot in Berkshire. Fitted with the personal plate that has been his for decades, 1 JYS, Stewart's chauffeur-driven Ford Scorpio makes sure he's on time for flights that in few years number less than a half-million miles.

His family is important to Jackie Stewart, but so are his professional interests. "When I sit in a racing car I find myself getting away from the whole world," he said in 1966. "It's literally like going on holiday. Obviously I'm delighted to have a family, but when I get into a racing car – and I think this applies to every racing driver – it's not that I shrug them off, it's just that I'm concentrating fully on something that demands 100 percent concentration." At SGP he's doing just that again. And it suits him.

Graham Gauld says the over-and-under shotgun isn't loaded when he and Jackie repair to a park in Glasgow's centre for some 1963 portraiture. Jackie, reserve to the two-man British Olympic shooting team in 1960, is wearing the official jacket of the British clay pigeon team. He still pursues trapshooting, the sport that has dominated Jackie's life like none other, at his Gleneagles school.

In 1963 Jackie relaxes with Graham Gauld in his own bungalow (right) and models his British trapshooting team jacket (far right).

Young Jackie watches brother Jimmy tweak his Healey Silverstone (left), which the latter races while doing his national service. The brothers grow up in the first bungalow to the left of the Dumbuck Garage (below) where Jackie plies his trade as a mechanic. At Charterhall in 1953 (bottom) a duffel-coated JYS aged 14 joins the Ecurie Ecosse mechanics and his brother Jimmy in flat cap at left.

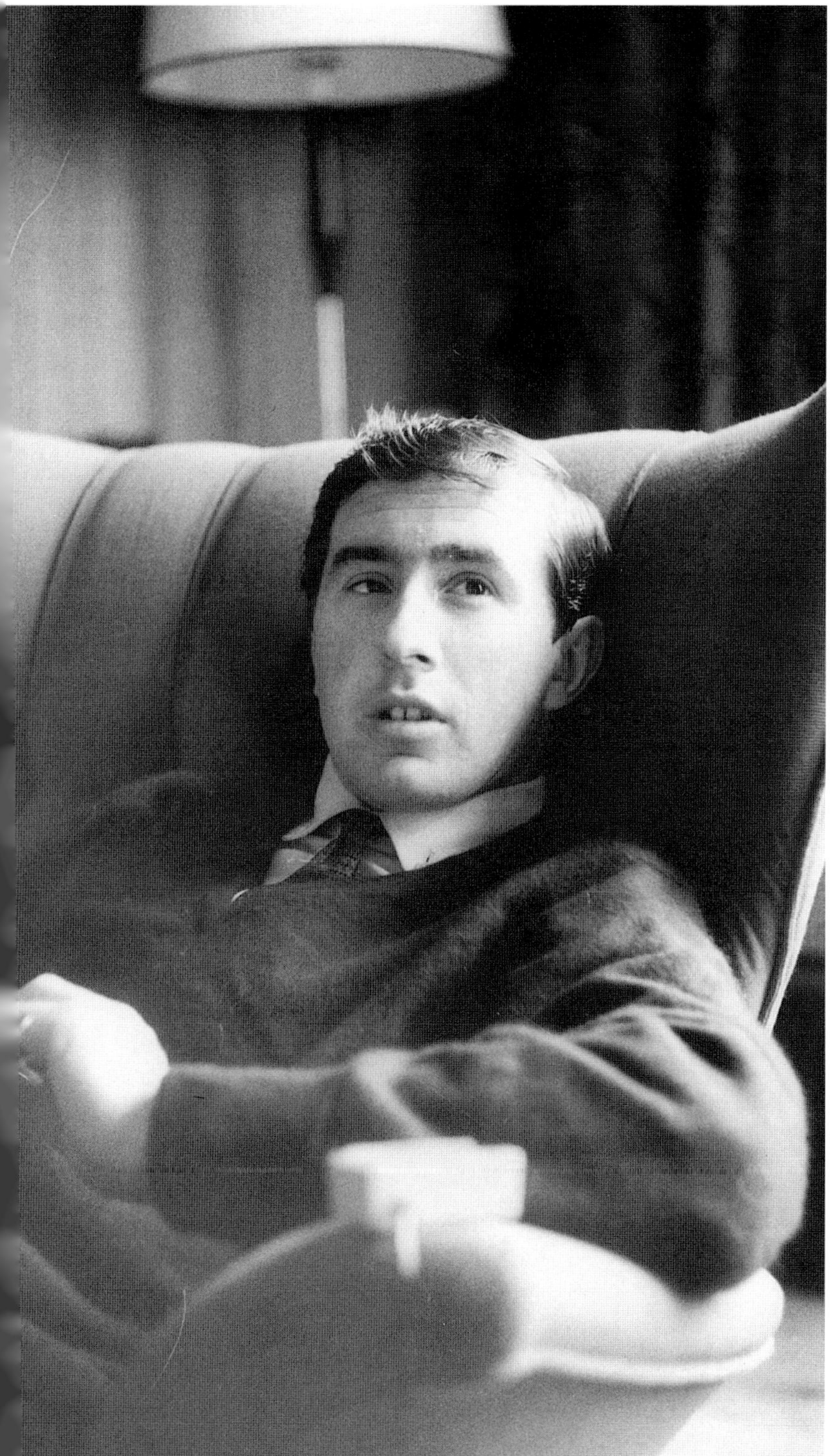

Lovely Helen McGregor is unimpressed when she first meets the younger Stewart heir but later judges him suitable; her parents at first reserve judgement. Jackie is beginning his commitment to racing when they marry in August 1962. The couple are close both at the races and on a seaside holiday.

The many faces of JYS. A hugely expressive individual, Jackie seldom leaves people in doubt about his desires and intentions. With the canniness of the Scot, however, he will reserve some of his cards for later in the game.

Jackie abjures the barber when he is unwell and finds wife Helen gazing admiringly at his Beatle-style locks. They, and his trademark fisherman's cap and sunglasses, become talismans for his success on the circuits.

Stewart interacts vividly with his colleagues on and off the track: an amused Jim Clark at Watkins Glen in 1966 (above); Lotus chief Colin Chapman, designer Maurice Philippe and Graham Hill at the 1967 Zandvoort debut of the Lotus 49 (top left); Graham and Bette Hill in the 'This Is Your Life' studio (centre left) and close friend and Swiss neighbour Jochen Rindt in 1967 (left).

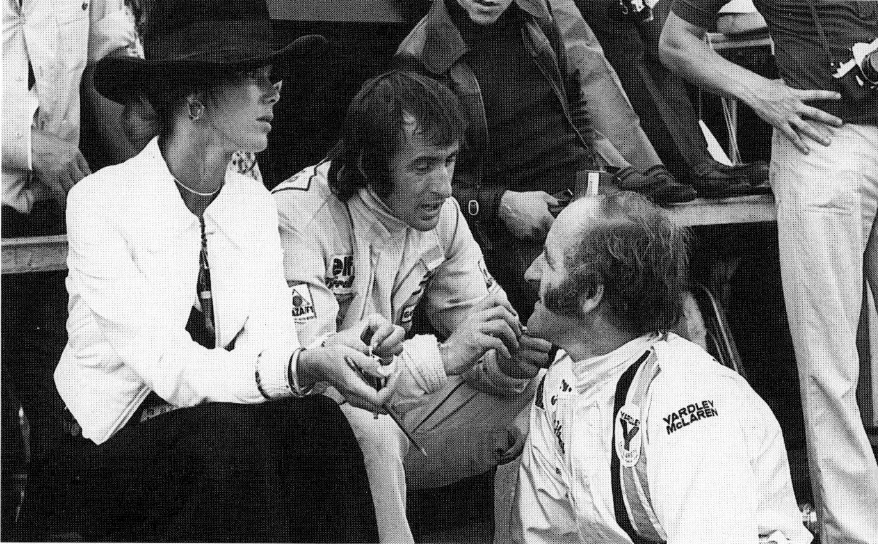

Photographer Max Le Grand and Stewart compare notes at Crystal Palace in 1970 (above). Max snaps JYS with David Hobbs (partly hidden) and John Surtees at the 1967 German Grand Prix (top right). With Helen, Jackie talks to Denny Hulme at Silverstone in 1973 (centre right). He meets Fangio at Monza in 1971 (right).

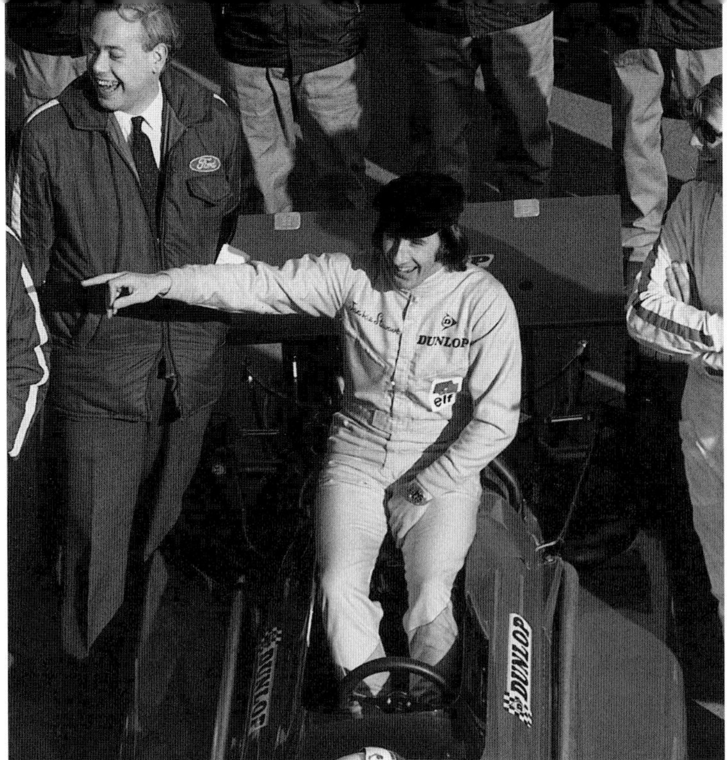

Clockwise with the demonstrative Jackie Stewart across two pages: Preparing to cycle to Brands Hatch for the 1964 British GP to avoid the traffic; amusing Cosworth designer Keith Duckworth with a jibe and gesture at the 1970 March launch; relishing his competitiveness in the Tyrrell Cooper-BMC in 1964; expressing relief and frowning behind his balaclava in 1970; admonishing Graham Gauld on the Brands Hatch grid in 1966.

elf
Ford

NAZA/2

Municipales
GOODYEAR
elf
Tyrrell-Ford
elf

CHAPTER 7

With Tyrrell to the top

Jackie Stewart felt that he had "a unique relationship" with Ken Tyrrell: "He made a great many decisions – but we were great arguers. I had his respect so I could argue with him, because I had won all these races." And Jackie did argue. "When things went wrong he sometimes complained over-much," said Tyrrell. "He tended to over-play it. But he only did it because he felt it made us do something about it." Stewart met his match in Tyrrell, whose fearsome verbal assaults were famously dubbed 'froth jobs' by his awed interlocutors.

"To me Ken is the complete team manager," Stewart elaborated. "He is full of sympathy when necessary, has all the dynamic attributes when required and is respected by other people in the sport. He has a bit of a temper too which is a good thing because you can be too nice and too soft with people. He puts himself 100 percent into the job and expects the same from everyone else, allowing no excuses for failure because there's always a good reason for a failure which could therefore have been avoided."

Yes, the sun does shine for Jackie Stewart and the Tyrrell-Ford racers through most of 1971, 1972 and 1973, starting with this victory – the first for a Tyrrell – in Barcelona's Montjuich Park on 18 April 1971.

The most competent team manager, however, is not at his best without a car, and that was Ken Tyrrell's position at the end of 1969. His Championship success and his loyalty to the Ford-Cosworth V-8 were rewarded by Ford's financial support of his team; Ford would help him buy new chassis. But what would they, could they, be?

Jean-Luc Lagardère had rejected an eleventh-hour appeal for his MS80. Goodyear, to which Brabham and McLaren were contracted, would object to a sale of a chassis by either operation to a Dunlop-shod team. Ken approached BRM, whose chassis could be adapted to the Ford V-8, but was turned down by Jackie's former employer. For all these teams, Ken reflected, "Stewart without a car wouldn't be opposition."

In one of those astonishing coincidences that make motor racing history – and it *was* only a coincidence –

a brash young team of motorsporting entrepreneurs had set up shop to make racing cars just when Tyrrell and Stewart needed some. Racing barrister Max Mosley, team manager Alan Rees, production expert Graham Coaker and engineer Robin Herd teamed up to build a Formula 1 car for Chris Amon, and if the initials of their surnames anagrammed as 'March' that was not a bad name for their car and company.

When the ambitious March venture was unveiled at a cold, windy Silverstone on 6 February 1970, a brand-new Dunlop-shod March 701 was ready to be demonstrated by Jackie Stewart. Wearing bold Elf decals, it was painted a dark blue that was subtly yet clearly consistent with Ford's backing of Tyrrell's team.

"They produced a car very quickly and very successfully," Jackie said of March, "to take pole position at the beginning of the season in South Africa, to finish third in the race, to win the Race of Champions at Brands Hatch, to win the Spanish Grand Prix, to sit on the pole at Monte Carlo. Around this time the opposition was napping pretty well, but unfortunately around May or June they began waking up. I was leading the World Championship, but then Jack Brabham took over, and then Jochen Rindt firmly took it over – winning four straight races in the new Lotus 72." Stewart ended the 1970 season equal fifth on points with Jack Brabham. March was third in the Constructors' league, after Lotus and Ferrari.

Jackie's chances of retaining his World Championship title had been wrecked by engine-related problems at the Grands Prix of Monaco, Belgium, Britain, Germany, Austria and the United States. In 1970, he said, Ford had "a bad season in Formula 1 in reliability. You must remember, however, that they made 69 Formula 1 engines. That's a lot of engines to build but it's a lot more to service. I think the standard of workmanship that was going into the servicing of these engines, during the middle part of the racing season, didn't really make for reliable motors."

We can be confident that Jackie's judgement, rendered so reasonably in public, was pithily communicated in private to Ford and Cosworth by Stewart and Tyrrell. Learning from this experience, Jackie said at the time, "Cosworth is only going to make ten engines in 1971 and these ten engines will be the only ones serviced by Cosworth. The rest of the engines for other teams will be farmed out to other builders, such as Lucas and Brian Hart." In fact Cosworth made 15 of its new 'Series 11' V-8s, two of which were allocated to Tyrrell.

This took care of the engines. But what about the chassis? It might be all right for a private team like Rob Walker or Jo Bonnier to buy last year's chassis from Lotus or McLaren but Tyrrell and Stewart had been at the top of the tree in 1969 and wished to continue looking down, not up, at the opposition. "Now I realised I had no choice," Tyrrell told Doug Nye. "I had to build my own car to become independent of an outside manufacturer and to ensure my drivers the best attention possible." This new direction was sought early in 1970, before they had even raced the new March, because their tests of the 701 had shown it to have little potential for development.

"This evening Ken asked me how I felt about his building us a car, something which wouldn't be ready until toward the end of the summer but might at least spare us a repetition of the situation we're now in," Jackie confided to his diary on 21 February 1970. "If it's fast, we'll run it for 1971. If not, it's just money. He said he's going to think about it, discuss design ideas with Derek Gardner, an Englishman with whom we worked last year on the Matra, take a look at his finances, and then get back to me. We're certainly going nowhere with the March."

Thirty-nine years old in 1970, Derek Gardner was a mechanical engineer who had been working on automatic transmissions before joining Ferguson Research, a Coventry company formed to exploit the four-wheel-drive concepts of Harry Ferguson and Freddie Dixon. There he found himself engineering the drive trains of Ferguson's own racing car and Ferguson projects for Indianapolis racers, including a

Novi and gas-turbine-powered Lotuses.

Unwittingly, Jackie Stewart had triggered Gardner's involvement with Tyrrell. A wave of enthusiasm for four-wheel-drive was sweeping the Grand Prix world in 1968, and Stewart was not immune to its appeal. Tyrrell and Matra should have one, he argued, because four-wheel drive would be dominant on wet tracks and might even be better on dry ones.

Matra agreed to build a simple tube-framed racing car for Tyrrell, the MS84, if Tyrrell would commission and fund its four-wheel-drive power train. Tyrrell did, from Ferguson: enter the quiet, serious, skilled, bushy-haired and racing-besotted Derek Gardner. The MS84 was never raced by Jackie although he practised with it six times during the 1969 season, which was as dry as 1968 had been wet. Nevertheless he and Tyrrell had met an impressive British engineer.

On 6 March Stewart diaried, as he and Peter Manso later published: "It's been decided, we're going to go with our own car. No-one knows about it except Derek Gardner, myself and Ken, and it's going to be kept a secret. Henceforth it is to be referred to as the SP, code for 'Secret Project.' Derek is back in England working on the design, a very simple design as I understand it, and he hopes to have a mockup in several weeks' time."

"Ken's requirements were few but firm," Gardner recalled. "The car had to be simple, competitive and there would be no time to develop it. It had to be right first time. He impressed on me the need to have the car built on schedule. He said if the car didn't race in the Gold Cup at Oulton Park, the whole project would be scrapped. We might as well throw it all in the Thames ..." The non-Championship Gold Cup would be held on 22 August, less than seven months from the evening early in February when Ken Tyrrell, in a pub at Henley-on-Thames, had actually asked Gardner to start work on the car. Only gradually had Ken broken the news to Jackie.

Someone else had to be in on Ken's secret. Building a new racing car would not be cheap. Tyrrell's strengthening relationship with Ford was the answer. Walter Hayes approved Ford's budgetary support of Ken's venture, which ultimately cost £22,500 – not petty cash in 1970. In return Tyrrell would have been willing to call the dark-blue car a 'Ford', but the final solution was to call it a 'Tyrrell-Ford', a designation carried by all the Tyrrell-built cars of this era.

Ford made its premises on Regent Street available for the presentation of the 'SP' on 17 August, in good time for the Gold Cup. During the summer Jackie had been to Derek Gardner's garage in Leamington Spa to try on his plywood-mockup cockpit for size; now he sat in the tub for the benefit of the press to show off a new racing car tailor-made to suit his 5ft 6½in and 148lbs. Savile Row, only a block away, could not have outfitted him better.

To say that the Tyrrell-Ford launch was a surprise would be to resort to grotesque understatement. Tyrrell's achievement knocked the racing establishment for six. It thought that it had successfully neutralised the cheeky Stewart challenge to the *status quo*, after the aberrant 1969 season. Yet here were Tyrrell and Stewart bouncing back with a car of their own, the work of an unknown designer. Could it possibly be any good? They wouldn't have to wait long to find out.

After his first lap at Oulton Park, said Derek Gardner, "Jackie rushed into the pits with the radiator full of grass and the throttle stuck open. That was put right in double quick time and he roared out to knock spots off the lap record which gave us the feeling that our new car did stand a chance." In fact Stewart slashed *two seconds* off the record to set fastest lap in a field that included Rindt and Hill in the latest Lotus 72s. He retired – engine failure as usual in 1970.

Jackie first raced the Tyrrell in a *Grande Epreuve* at St. Jovite in Canada, where he put it on pole in the last lap of the last session and led the pack until the bumpy track broke a stub axle a third of the way through the race. Derek Gardner had redesigned front uprights ready for Watkins Glen, where Stewart – again qualifying on the front row – raced away from the field, including, to his surprise, the rejuvenated

Ferraris of Ickx and Regazzoni.

"In the race Stewart shot off and built up a really fantastic lead over the Ferraris," wrote Jack Brabham. "I got completely demoralised because Stewart lapped me – he passed me on the straight going so quickly it was just a joke. He looked out of the car and gave me a little wave, as if to say, 'Come on, get out of fourth gear or whatever it is' – and just disappeared into the blue. He should have won that race easily but his engine started to smoke and finally ran out of oil." In the 1970 season's last race at Mexico City Jackie held second place before pitting to refit a steering-column bushing and retiring after hitting a large stray dog.

Here were performances that augured well for success in 1971 after the frustrations of 1970. Ken Tyrrell had made a massive effort to create equipment that would retain his star driver. After the tragic death of his friend Jochen Rindt, posthumous 1970 World Champion – which followed the fatal accidents that summer of both Piers Courage and Bruce McLaren – Jackie had no challenger as the best and most complete racing driver. And he was free to move if he wanted to. Ferrari's new 312B with its flat-12 engine was shaping up as a formidable opponent. Ferrari was certainly among the half-dozen Formula 1 teams that extended attractive offers to Stewart for 1971. But calling himself "an old woman about switching from something I know," Stewart elected to stay with Tyrrell.

Big changes came in 1971. Ford reduced its racing support and Ken reconstituted his team as Elf-Team Tyrrell with the support of the French oil company that had done so well out of its association with Jackie in his 1969 Championship year. Dunlop withdrew from Formula 1 and Goodyear took its place at Tyrrell, also signing a separate agreement with Stewart. And Derek Gardner built another Tyrrell-Ford for a team-mate who had joined Tyrrell at the end of 1970: French Grand Prix debutant François Cévert. Much taller than Jackie, the strikingly good-looking Cévert needed a tub four inches longer.

"Nineteen seventy-one brought a busier season than ever before," Stewart reflected. "I competed in the North American Can-Am series, as well as the Grand Prix season. From June to October I was commuting once a week to North America from Europe, simply to race. I ended up with a duodenal ulcer, but I did win two Can-Am races, finished third in the series and won the World Championship." In achieving the latter he came close to matching his 1969 pace by winning five of the first seven of the 1971 season's *Grandes Epreuves*.

In one of the two that he didn't win, the first race of the year at Kyalami, Jackie placed second behind Mario Andretti's Ferrari in a Tyrrell that had been hastily rebuilt after crashing, with a stuck throttle, ending almost 1,400 miles of tyre testing with Goodyear that led to the introduction of slick treads and also suggested that Cosworth had got to grips with its reliability problems. In his second non-winning outing, at a rainy Zandvoort, Jackie this time found himself on the wrong end of the wet-weather stick. Struggling with balky brakes, he suffered the mortification of being lapped five times by Ickx's winning Ferrari and finishing eleventh.

Victories came in Spain – the first win for a Tyrrell-Ford – Monaco, France, Britain and Germany. The French and German races saw dream finishes for Tyrrell that set the seal on the excellence of Derek Gardner's design: Stewart first and Cévert second. This accelerated the accumulation of points that brought Tyrrell the 1971 Manufacturers' Championship with more than double the total of runner-up BRM. After the British race the Italian-inspired pit-lane gossip that Stewart must be running a $3^1/2$-litre engine was silenced after his Cosworth V-8 was stripped and found to be a legal three litres.

Jackie lost a rear wheel in the Austrian race, crashing without injury, and engine failure finally caught up with him at Monza. At Mosport in Canada he was in the lead when a chaotic race was declared completed at 60 percent distance on account of rain and mist. Jackie's setup didn't suit his Goodyears in the season's last Championship race at Watkins Glen, where he finished fifth, but François Cévert won to collect the traditionally-generous Glen purse for Tyrrell.

As a matched set with the 1971 World Championship, which he clinched when Jacky Ickx failed to finish in Austria, Stewart had seven pole positions and three fastest laps to show for his season, one of the most dominant that any Grand Prix driver has ever enjoyed. He was also exhausted and suffering from mononucleosis. Nor did his sponsor and appearance commitments give him much chance to recharge himself: "The repercussions of winning the Championship did not allow me to put my feet up when the season ended, so by the end of the year I was a very tired wee boy. With the constant time and zone changes I had become numbed, and what Helen called 'a vegetable'."

Expert at keeping his secrets, unwilling to offer a sliver of encouragement to his rivals, Jackie showed no glimmer of his fatigued condition at Buenos Aires in January 1972 for the return to the calendar of the Argentine Grand Prix. He sat on the front row, led from flag to flag and set fastest lap. Here was a gauntlet flung down to challenge any and all who thought they could catch the double Champion.

Stewart put in his usual stalwart tyre-testing siege at Kyalami before the South African Grand Prix in early March. There he led from pole until forced out with an oil-less gearbox on lap 45. In the next races at Jarama and Monaco, Stewart was visibly under pressure, more the numbed 'vegetable' than his usual confident self in both practice and the race. The first saw a win by rising star Emerson Fittipaldi in the Lotus 72; the second a victory in a wet race by former Matra team-mate Jean-Pierre Beltoise driving a BRM. It was the last win that would ever be enjoyed by the marque that introduced Jackie Stewart to Grand Prix racing.

"Stewart was feeling very unhappy and unwell after the long, wet race" at Monaco, wrote Doug Nye, "and felt too dizzy to drive in a test session the following week at Nivelles – venue of the Belgian GP – which was in any case rained off. He was sure something was seriously wrong." The doctors agreed: "My ulcer was discovered to be bleeding which came as no surprise to some people. It meant six weeks without racing and more time than I had ever had before with Helen and my two sons. It was great. I was on about ten pills a day and I was so heavily sedated and gaga that it was terrific – I loved it. I didn't even go and look at television if there was a race on. I even missed Wimbledon, something I never do."

From mid-May of 1972 to the beginning of July Jackie Stewart took this break from racing on doctor's orders. While recuperating at Clayton House he received devastating news: "On 11 June 1972 – my birthday – Jo Bonnier was killed at Le Mans. Once again [like Rindt] it was a tragedy close to home. Jo had been more to do with choosing Switzerland as our home than anyone. His two sons went to school with Paul and Mark, and I took space in Jo's office complex. He was also the man who had worked harder than any other in the interest of safety in motor racing, and now he had been killed."

Jackie's ability to compartmentalise his thoughts and emotions came to the rescue again, as it had when he raced at Monza after Rindt's death in practice. He returned to competition in the French Grand Prix at Clermont-Ferrand on 2 July and, benefiting from a puncture to Chris Amon's Matra, took the lead and held it. At Brands Hatch, after setting fastest lap Jackie was only four seconds behind winner Fittipaldi, but the maturing Brazilian had been building up an unassailable Championship points lead.

Meanwhile back at Ockham, where Ken Tyrrell was installing handsome new workshops to supplement his huts and Portakabins, Derek Gardner had been building a new Tyrrell-Ford. Even lower and shorter than the original, the 005 had better aerodynamics and provision for inboard-mounted front brakes. Jackie had no luck with it at Austria or Monza, but used the 005 to storm the end-of-season races at Mosport and Watkins Glen, setting fastest laps for good measure.

This performance served fair warning to the opposition that Jackie Stewart was not yet ready to hang up his helmet. The 1973 season was a long one: 15 races from 28 January to 7 October. Jackie Stewart competed in every race but the last. He won five: the Grands Prix of South Africa, Belgium, Monaco, Holland and Germany. With second places in Brazil and Austria and third in Argentina this was enough to win for Stewart his third World Championship ahead of youngsters Emerson Fittipaldi and Ronnie Peterson.

Jackie clinched the Championship at Monza with a lowly fourth place in a race he considers one of the best of his career. Stopping early to change a punctured tyre, he plummeted from his early fourth place to nineteenth. "I'd had an early pit stop, lost a lap, and then got my head down," said Jackie. "The thing about that place is that it's so easy – I mean, *anyone* can go quickly at Monza. So therefore it was much more difficult to gain ground there. You had to be technically perfect, clinical and clean, because otherwise you scrubbed off speed. That drive was dictated entirely by my head, and it was as good as ever I did, I believe." Just eight laps from the finish he was back in fourth again.

In one of those cruel ironies that only motor racing can offer, the final race of the season at Watkins Glen, which would have been Jackie's hundredth Grand Prix, was not contested because Elf-Team Tyrrell withdrew after the death in practice of the 1971 Glen winner, the hugely-popular François Cévert. A week later Jackie announced what he had known since April: that the Glen event was to be his last.

"I worked over the facts in my mind for some time," Stewart said later. "Finally it all came together. I arranged a meeting with Walter Hayes and John Waddell of Ford Motor Company on 5 April. I committed myself to retiring after the United States Grand Prix on 7 October. No-one else was to know except Ken Tyrrell – least of all Helen. I did not want her to be involved in a ten-green-bottles-sitting-on-the-wall scene, waiting for the last green bottle to come down at Watkins Glen in October. The next day, 6 April, I was driven by Ken Tyrrell from London to his workshops in Surrey, and this gave me the chance to tell him of my decision. I was happy to get it off my chest."

The official announcement came on 14 October: "I did feel a bit lightheaded that day. There was a sense of relief, but also regret. If things had ended a little more happily, in fact, the regret might have been more in my mind. We'd intended to do the announcement a week after my last race. The way it worked out, though, it was a week after François' accident, three days after his funeral ..."

A man at the height of his powers in a racing car engineered specifically to his requirements prepared and entered by a team dedicated to his World Championship success – what can only be a dream for most racing drivers is achieved by Stewart with Tyrrell.

GOODYEAR
elf
NAZA/F1
NAZA/F1
elf

At the launch of the March racing cars and company at Silverstone in February 1970 the author snaps Stewart in conversation with Dick Jeffrey of Dunlop, the new Tyrrell-entered March-Ford 701 on the move and a pensive Jackie already musing on the inadequacies of the car he is committed to drive that season.

He scores March's sole victory in a Grande Epreuve *at Spain's Jarama in April, passing the burning wreck of Jackie Oliver's BRM which T-bones Ickx's Ferrari on the first lap. Oliver escapes injury, while Ickx suffers minor burns.*

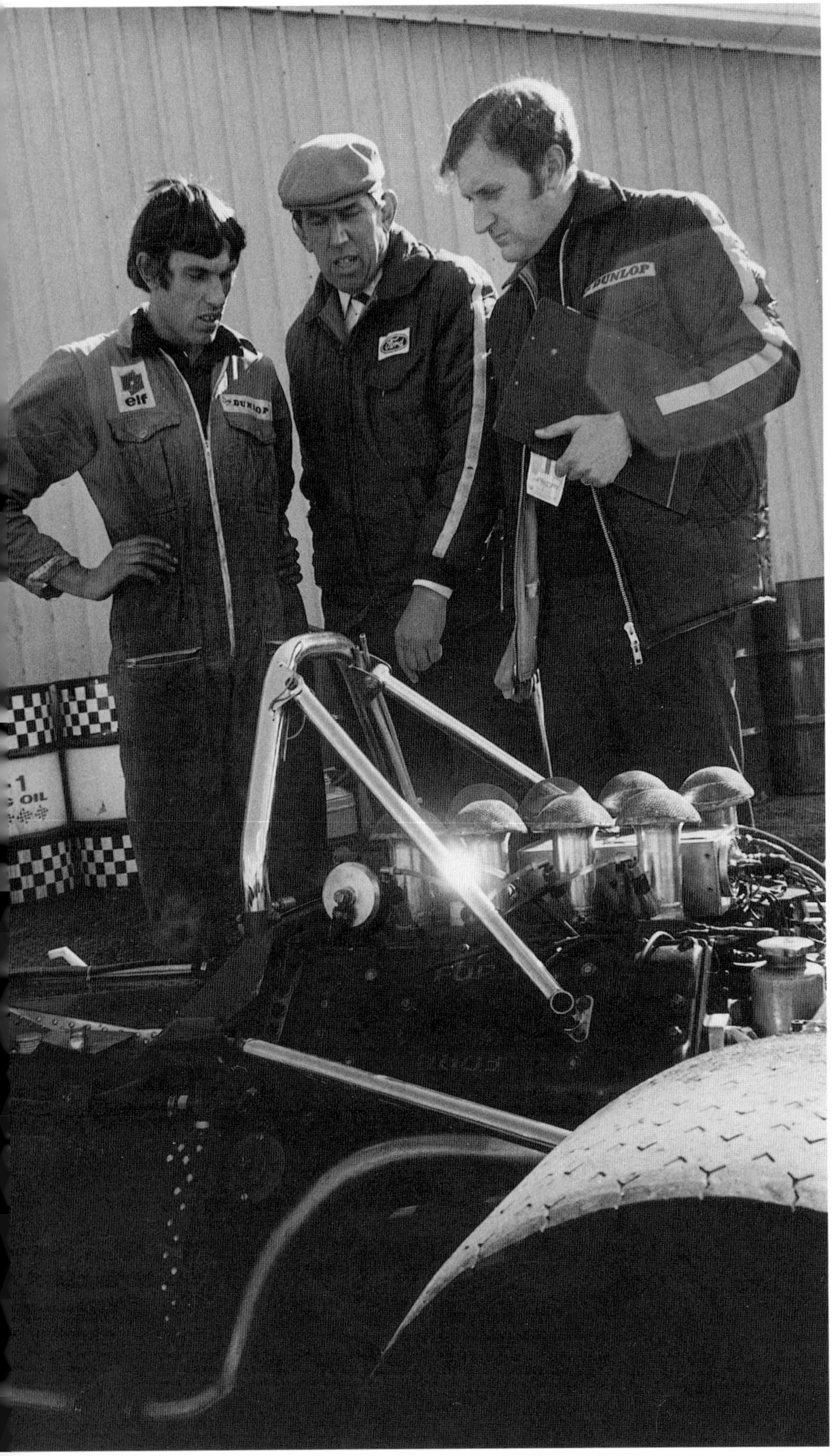
elf
DUNLOP
DUNLOP

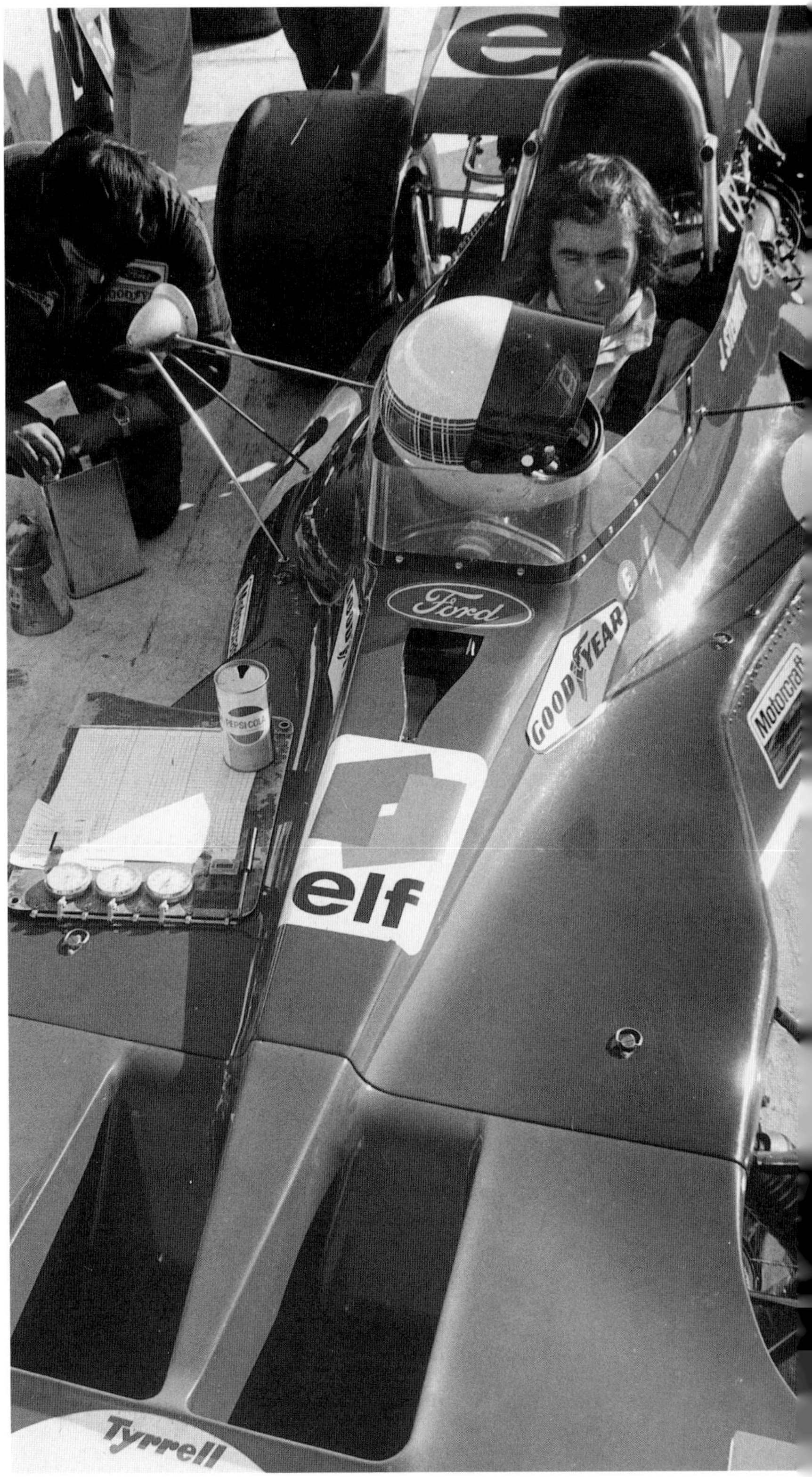
Ford
GOOD YEAR
Motorcraft
elf
Tyrrell

Key members of the Stewart support team are (far left, left to right) mechanic Roger Hill, team owner Ken Tyrrell and designer Derek Gardner. JYS stays put while Tyrrell-Ford 003 is fed and watered at Watkins Glen in 1971 (near left). An inkling of the potential of Tyrrell-Ford 001 is revealed on the first lap of the 1970 US Grand Prix (above). Jackie has to give best to Clay Regazzoni's Ferrari in the March 1971 Race of Champions at Brands Hatch (below and overleaf).

STEWART
GOODYEAR
elf
Tyrrell

GOODYEAR
Autolite

Ford
FORD
GOODYEAR
elf
Tyrrell
8
Motorcraft
Ford

elf
1
Tyrrell
Ford
GOODYEAR

Jackie races the original Tyrrell-Ford with its hammerhead-wing nose (above) at Monaco in 1971, where he wins from pole and sets a new lap record, and with a "sports-car" nose at Monaco in 1972 (left bottom) placing fourth and at Watkins Glen in 1971 (left top) finishing fifth.

On the old Nürburgring, a track he loathes, Stewart nevertheless is victorious in his last two Championship years. Left to right, he is joined by Clay Regazzoni and François Cévert in 1971 (above) and by Cévert, Tyrrell and Jacky Ickx in 1973 (below). Helen shares the limelight both years as does Price Metternich of the FIA.

The Tyrrell-Stewart dialogue continues to yield results in the early 1970s (above left and right). Celebrations are in order (below left) when Stewart and Cévert place one–two in the 1973 Belgian GP with the young Frenchman getting fastest lap. When Jackie seals his 1973 Championship with a fourth at Monza, Goodyear's Leo Mehl joins the party.

GOODYEAR
elf
Tyrrell
1

GOODYEAR

The flat-12 Ferraris often threaten in 1971 but Stewart and Tyrrell sweep them aside to take both Driver's and Constructor's World Championships. JYS powers ahead of Regazzoni (5) and Ickx (4) at Paul Ricard to win the French GP (above) and runs in second, holding off Regazzoni's Ferrari (5) and team-mate Cévert, in the Austrian GP (below) before losing a wheel and retiring. Stewart is in third place (preceding pages) when October's celebratory World Championship Victory Race at Brands Hatch is stopped after 15 of 40 laps when Jo Siffert tragically crashes and is killed.

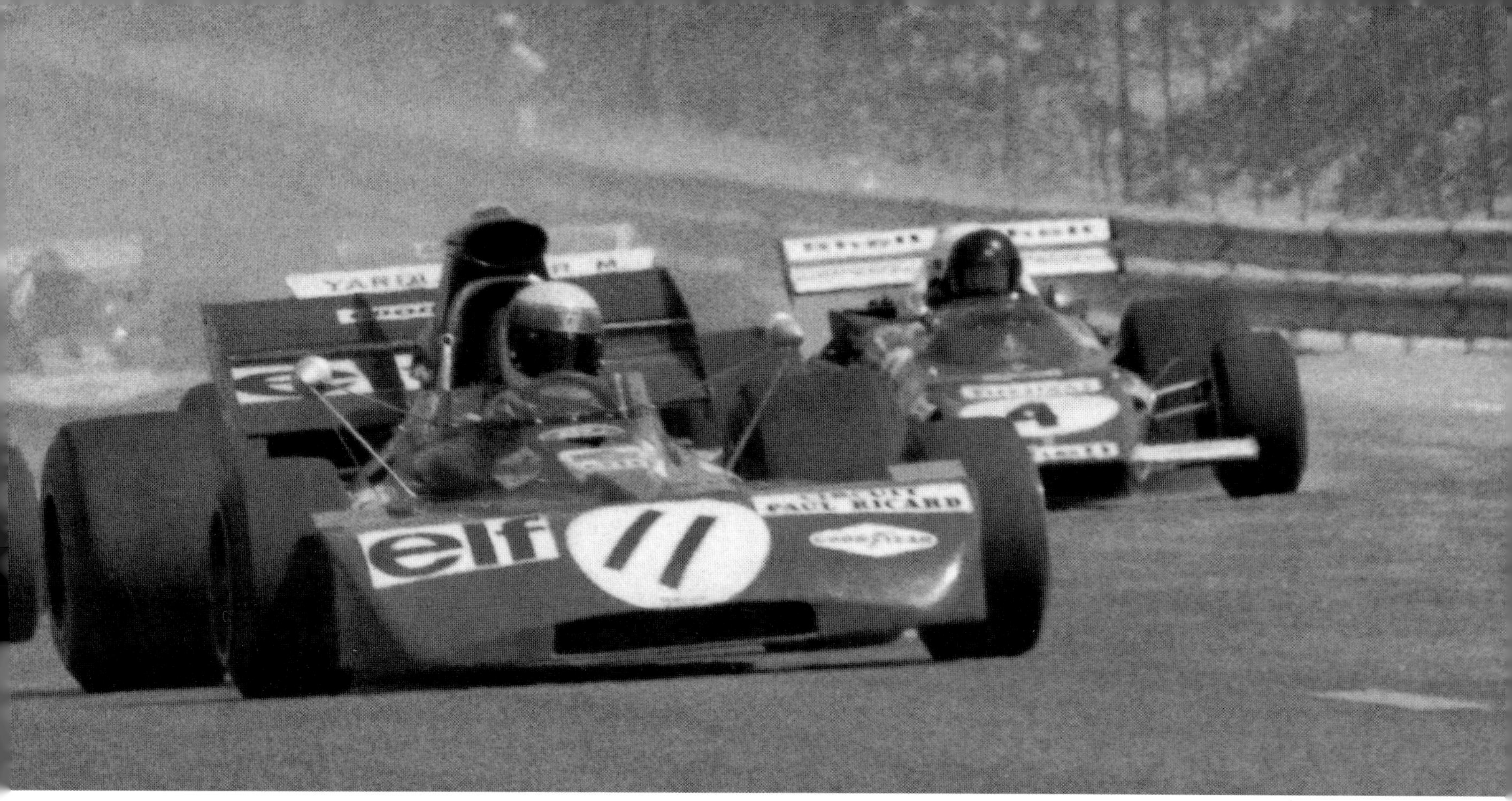
PAUL RICARD
elf
11
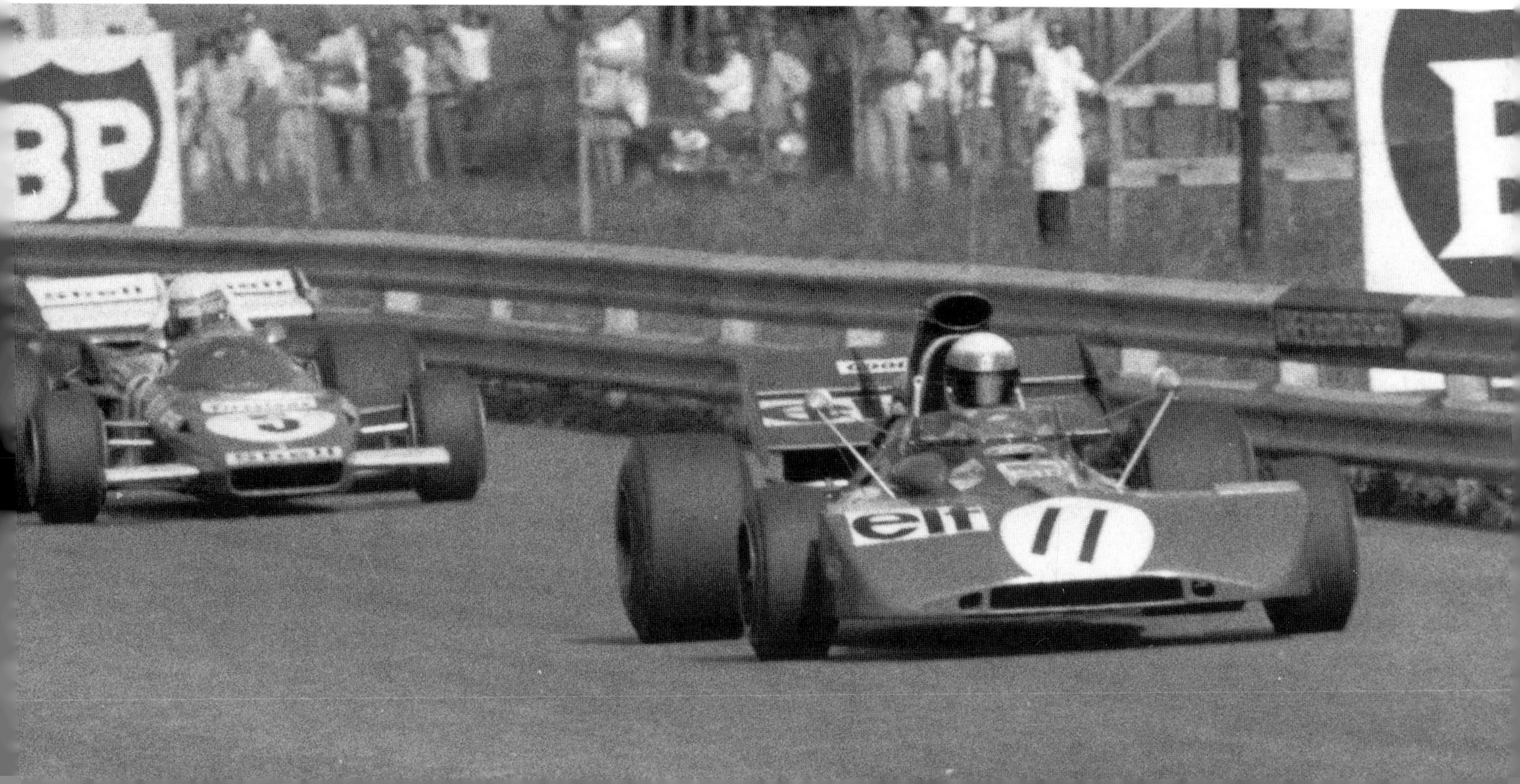
BP
elf
11

Brian Redman's McLaren trails Jackie in the wet 1972 Monaco Grand Prix (above). Wet electrics in his Cosworth-Ford engine drop Stewart to a fourth-place finish. At Barcelona in Spain in 1973 he flies high (below) in Tyrrell 006/2 but is forced out by brake problems.

Stewart is about to overtake Cévert to finish fourth in the 1973 Italian GP (above) during his epic drive from the tail of the field. Monte Carlo's tunnel (below) is a backdrop to Jackie's winning race there in 1973, the year he places fifth at Sweden's Anderstorp (overleaf).

GOODYEAR
elf
5

STEWART
Ford
elf
Tyrrell
Ford
GOODYEAR

DUNLO

CHAPTER 8

Speed king at Monaco

For flat racing it's Epsom or the Kentucky Derby, for soccer Wembley Stadium, for tennis Wimbledon, for golf the Masters at Augusta and for American football the Super Bowl – wherever it is. If motor racing has an all-star showplace, and it does, then it is the annual Grand Prix in the city of Monte Carlo in the principality of Monaco.

The race around the streets of Monte Carlo is in the rich tradition of the earliest years of motorsport. At the beginning of the 20th Century people wealthy enough to afford a motor car wintered in the south of France, in Monaco or nearby at Nice or Cannes on the Côte d'Azur. "From November to March," wrote W. F. Bradley, "these three towns attracted the royalty, the aristocracy, the wealthy of the entire world." *Ergo* it was a good place to sell them a car. So in January 1897, to flaunt the performance of the latest models, a race was organised from Monte Carlo to Marseilles and back. The winner averaged 19mph.

Is it a Churchillian 'V for victory' or a reminder that Monaco 1966 was his second victory in a Grande Epreuve? *Either way Jackie's gesture is appropriate as he and Helen greet the crowds on their begarlanded tour of honour.*

For Monte Carlo, with rocky topography that seemed unsuited to car competitions, the sea was its first real venue for speed. For a decade from 1904 power-boat racing was the sport that attracted the wealthy, using the same engines that powered the racing cars of the day. Then in 1914 the first Schneider Cup race for seaplanes was held from the Monte Carlo harbour. Motorsporting needs were addressed in 1911, when the Monte Carlo Rally was first staged for competitors starting from far-flung cities in Europe and converging on the warmer January climate of the Côte d'Azur. After its revival in 1924 this became and remains one of the great motor-sport classics.

The auto race through the streets of Monte Carlo was a 1929 brainstorm of Antony Noghès, who saw it as the event he needed to enhance the prestige of the Automobile Club de Monaco so that it could qualify for entry into the hallowed halls of the international federation of motoring clubs, the FIA. "For days on end," he told David Hodges, "I went over the avenues of the Principality until I hit on the only possible circuit. Today, the roads comprising this circuit look as though they were made for the purpose. But then! Some of the obstacles seemed to be insuperable – the steps near the Bureau de Tabac, for example, had to be replaced by an inclined plane connecting the Quai des Etats Unis with the Quai Albert Premier."

"Wonderful, marvellous, stupendous," raved racing driver and Monte Carlo resident Louis Chiron when he heard of the Noghès plan. The inevitable objections were overcome and the Principality prevailed with the high level of organisation that it has managed ever since. The first Grand Prix of Monaco, raced in April 1929, saw a Bugatti victory and stamped the seal of success on this unique event. Its validity was confirmed in 1934 when His Serene Highness Prince Louis II of Monaco was joined in the royal grandstand by Sweden's King Gustave, Spain's King Alfonso XIII and Romania's King Nicholas – no mean racer himself.

There were obvious limitations to a twisty two-mile course composed of a peculiar assortment of local roads and seafront esplanades, and a venue that made it very difficult to charge admission to spectators. But the Monte Carlo circuit continued to weave its fascination for the Grand Prix circus after the Second World War. Most years saw races there, although a 1952 experiment to convert the event to sports cars was not repeated. One of Jackie's mentors, Graham Hill, made a speciality of winning the race. He managed it five times.

Apart from the introduction of chicanes at various points and the lengthening of the tunnel to suit the building of a hotel above it, the glamorous and mountainous Monte Carlo circuit has altered little over the years – further enhancing its mesmerising aura of history and tradition. The biggest change, which took its length from just under to just over two miles, was made for 1973, the last year Stewart raced there. This comprised a new seafront road that zigzagged around the swimming pool and an extension of the old Gasworks Hairpin to create the La Rascasse series of corners that decants the cars into the finishing straight.

The Grand Prix of Monaco is a stellar enough event for a racing weekend. But it usually has a supporting race or two. Traditionally, in the modern era that has been for Formula Junior and then for Formula 3 cars. Of all the races on the calendar, this is seen as one of the most influential for a young driver's career because it is staged under the talent-sniffing noses of the Formula 1 team owners and managers.

In 1964 the Formula 3 race was run in two heats and a final. During the first practice, said *The Autocar*, "that meteoric Scotsman Jackie Stewart was some five seconds faster than anyone else, in the Ken Tyrrell Cooper-BMC." No one was closer to Jackie in final practice than two seconds, and he comfortably won his first heat. In the final, Argentine Silvio Moser, the second-heat winner in a Brabham, tried on a challenge but Stewart took the lead on the third of 24 laps and finished with 20 seconds in hand over the highly-touted Moser, an eternity in Formula 3 terms.

"I watched the F3 race from Eddie Hall's flat above the new start line," said BRM's Tony Rudd of his Monte Carlo visit in 1964. "It was the perfect way to go motor racing. The ladies could freshen up, there were wonderful things to eat, and absolutely fearsome gin and tonics. As I watched the race, which had got underway before I arrived, one car was either very badly last, or an awfully long way in the lead. I borrowed Eddie's binoculars and watched. It was a certain J. Y. Stewart. He was very smooth and obviously in a class of his own."

Twelve months later, having chosen BRM from the several Formula 1 offers his Formula 3 performance had inspired, J. Y. Stewart was tucked into the cockpit of one of Tony Rudd's immaculate dark-green racers. For a newcomer to this class of racing his form was excellent, placing him third on the grid less than half a second behind polesitter Graham Hill and Jack Brabham. Jim Clark and Dan Gurney were giving the race a miss to compete for dollars at Indianapolis.

Hill and Stewart roared into the race lead in that order, and when Hill had to use an escape road to avoid another competitor Jackie found himself leading the GP of Monaco on his first attempt. Five laps later, however, at the fast St. Devote bend at the foot of the hill that climbs to the casino, his BRM lurched into a wild spin backwards up the hill and onto the pavement. Luckily the resulting damage was mild enough to let him carry on. Graham battled his way up to the front again, where he finished, and Stewart came home third behind Lorenzo Bandini's flat-12 Ferrari.

"Over his head," murmured the railbirds of Stewart's big spin while leading the race. "He threw it all away," opined Denis Jenkinson. Stewart wouldn't be 26 until next month; the youngster was all right in Formula 3 but not yet up to Formula 1, they said. Anything but, rejoined Jackie: "My spin at Monaco wasn't a case of over-exuberance, or the car getting the better of me. I'd just won at Silverstone having driven what I thought was a steady race while staying ahead of Surtees rather than settling down behind the Ferrari and following John home. At Monaco I hit oil. It was as simple as that. Okay, I should have been able to get myself out of it, but I *was* a new driver. I wasn't expected to know all the tricks of the trade."

The magic allure of the Monegasque circuit and its exotic environment were already weaving their enchantment for Stewart: "There are other Grand Prix races which are exciting and steeped in atmosphere, but none so completely and in so many ways as Monte Carlo. The harbour, the Mediterranean, the palm trees and the old town itself all mix and blend with the modern to give a feeling of nostalgia and change, above all a sense of intimacy, as though everything somehow still belongs here and will remain part of the place perhaps forever."

Change came to Grand Prix racing in 1966 with a new Formula 1 that allowed three-litre unsupercharged engines; BRM was preparing its exotic H-16. This was not race-ready in May, however, although BRM brought one along to Monaco. Instead Tony Rudd gave Graham Hill and Jackie Stewart their 1965 cars with V-8 engines enlarged to two litres. These, as it happened, were just the ticket for the twisty Monte Carlo track. Stewart was third on the grid, just a tenth of a second ahead of Hill in fourth place.

Jim Clark was on pole with a similarly-adapted 1965 Lotus-Climax but had trouble shifting out of his special starting gear and never figured in the race. John Surtees led in the new V-12 Ferrari until the transmission broke after 16 laps, leaving – in the lead – J. Y. Stewart. His serene progress to the chequered flag to score his second *Grande Epreuve* victory and his first at Monaco was unthreatened by Bandini who finished 40 seconds later.

This was a masterful win by Jackie, who led laps 15 to 100. In fact he was half-way through his exultant tour of honour in an open course car when he remembered that this wasn't, in fact, his first Grand Prix victory. His win at Monza the year before had come so late in the race that he hadn't had time to savour it. This time he did. And his success was shared by millions of Americans who watched the race on ABC Sports television, lured to Europe by Ford's all-out campaign at Le Mans.

Towards the late 1960s Jackie and Helen Stewart were coming to know better the Rainiers, Monaco's remarkable ruling family. "We'd been invited to the Palace by Prince Rainier for drinks at ten," Stewart said of the first such occasion. "I'd always wanted to see the Palace but had never been there, and now we've gone by invitation. Prince Rainier and his wife greeted us and I was particularly impressed with Princess Grace, an incredibly beautiful woman who seems ageless, still retains an American accent, and is immune from affectation, yet stately. Her husband is habitually dressed in a sombre blue, single-breasted suit and he carries himself not with his shoulders back, his head proud, but rather slumps.

"When I first met him some years ago I was intimidated, but it was soon clear that he didn't want me to bow or curtsy, or any of that. Still, I've never wanted to be completely familiar. There are grounds for familiarity, sure, not the least of which is the Prince's passion for cars and racing. He keeps an extensive collection of vintage cars in the Palace garage and takes very seriously the Principality's Grand Prix."

As well as getting to know Monaco's royalty, Jackie was getting to know its extraordinary circuit. "For some reason," he said, "cars never seem to react naturally at Monte Carlo. It's a very special place, and the only way to get the best from a car here is to follow it rather than lead it, make allowances and drive around its problems rather than trying to dominate them. If you're overly nervous or pushy, trouble is inevitable.

"Every year at Monte Carlo it takes a day or so to scrub the track, because in some parts it is quite dusty and has no bite to it. Similarly, you need to treat the first lap or two of the race with respect because the dust comes back in a limited way every night, particularly down on the waterfront near the Chicane. The surface here can change quite a lot from day to day. Of all the tracks I know, I go slower on my first lap at Monte Carlo than anywhere else.

"It is a great race to win because you can have such a celebration; or lose because it is such an easy place to get over the disappointment quickly." At the end of the 1960s this became a philosophy of no small value to the speedy Scot. Four straight Monaco Grands Prix passed without Stewart there at the finish.

Although Jackie, now team leader for BRM, had one of the H-16s at his disposal for the 1967 Monaco race, he elected to drive a V-8 much like the one he'd used to win the previous year, enlarged to 2.1-litres. The pace of progress of the three-litre cars meant that Stewart qualified only sixth fastest but on the seventh lap he passed Denny Hulme's Brabham-Repco to take a commanding lead. Eight laps, later, however, the BRM's final-drive gears failed and he was out.

Denny Hulme was the winner. The popular Lorenzo Bandini should have been second but, late in the race, made a minor error of judgement that sent his Ferrari bouncing across the esplanade. It overturned, bursting into fire. The rescue crew were slow to react and Bandini lay trapped, horrendously burned and injured. Italy's best racing driver by far died three days later of his injuries. Concerns about the safety of racing, already great, were intensified by this tragedy.

Nineteen sixty-eight was one of Jackie Stewart's most frustrating years at Monte Carlo because – sidelined through injury – he could only stand and watch his car, the Tyrrell-entered Matra-Ford that should have been the race winner, driven into retirement by Johnny Servoz-Gavin. The young Frenchman, in only his second Grand Prix, qualified the blue Matra on the front row just slower than Graham Hill's Lotus-Ford and leapt into the lead at the start.

Both Tyrrell and Stewart had done all they could to settle down Servoz-Gavin but the excitement of leading in front of a friendly and enthusiastic home crowd worked against them. On his fourth lap Johnny touched a barrier, which led to a drive shaft breakage and a crash. In a field so severely decimated that only five cars were still running during the last three-quarters of the race, Graham Hill was the winner.

In no other race is the driver so aware of the spectators and their interest in his progress. "The crowd consists of Frenchmen, Italians, Spaniards, people from all over Europe cheering and shouting, waving from the balconies that are tiered, like so many steps, up the sides of the hills," said Jackie Stewart. "There are more people watching from yachts at anchor in the harbour and countless others lining the streets and hanging out of café windows waiting for the start."

People are drawn to Formula 1 racing, said Stewart, by "the glamour, the colour, the excitement. For sponsors the demographics are very positive. The lifestyles of the rich and famous, if you like, particularly at a place like Monaco. And the affluence that surrounds it is far in excess of anything that occurs in any other sport, even Royal Ascot or the Kentucky Derby. Even the richest events don't have the kind of style or opulence and class that you get in Grand Prix racing."

Nothing tops royalty for class, and since getting to know the Rainiers Jackie has helped many of Europe's royals understand the arcane world of motorsports.

King Juan Carlos of Spain, a great auto enthusiast, is a friend, as is Greece's exiled King Constantine. Among Britain's royal family the Princess Royal has been particularly close to Stewart. No figure in motorsports has more open or welcome access to the House of Windsor.

"Formula 1 attracts what I call professional spectators, some who have been in it as long as I have," says Stewart. "And they're very professional. They know how to get the right credentials. They know how to get the best tables in the restaurants where the Grand Prix insiders go. They know everybody who's important. They survive because they're not a threat to anyone. They're just nice people. And they're completely engrossed and in love with the sport. With Formula 1. They love going to the pits, and maybe walking round part of the track, seeing and being seen. And looking comfortable, not obtrusive, and not being a bother to anybody.

"They love the excitement. I don't care how many times you've been to a Grand Prix, you still feel the calm before the storm at the start, and that's very special. Everybody feels it – the drivers, their wives, the team managers. Everybody wants to look cool, calm and collected and they're not. They're scared, and they're highly strung and there's a tension in the air, which is electric. There's nothing like it to get the adrenalin pumping."

Jackie shed his own spectator status at Monaco in 1969 when he put his Matra-Ford MS80 on pole and shared the front row with Chris Amon's Ferrari. Only one more time would Stewart *not* be on pole at Monaco. He had to set his quick time on the second qualifying day because the authorities, after inspecting the high-flying wings attached to the cars' suspensions on Thursday, banned all aerodynamic devices that were not attached to the body and nullified the first day's times.

Stewart segued smoothly from pole into the lead on race day but in so doing he was all too aware that his race might be a short one. "During the morning of race day," wrote Jabby Crombac, "it was found that the universal joints in the transmission had cracked, as they had already done in practice, and there were no replacements available on the spot. Both cars broke this component in the same lap." Jackie backed off when Chris Amon retired but not enough to save a flawed part. Graham Hill collected another of his Monaco wins.

"It was not a hard race," Jackie recalled of 1969. "In fact, it was particularly easy because the car was handling so well; I suppose I was driving at around seven-tenths during the race even from the first laps which made me slightly anxious. I was running at reduced revs, and I was only using about 8,500 or 9,000 at the maximum which is 1,000 rpm less than I normally use. I was avoiding the bumps, I was not hitting any kerbs, and I was driving off the waterfront without actually going up on the pavement to avoid jolting down again to save giving the transmission a bit of a jolt on the approach to the tunnel, in fact doing all the things that I felt I could do to save the car, but of course a universal joint broke."

When Stewart failed to finish yet again in 1970 he was accused of car-breaking, a charge he had good reason to refute. "For two years now they've criticised me for driving too hard at Monaco," he said, "but it's all a lot of rubbish. I've never had quieter or easier races than at Monaco. No effort. No strain on the car. Keeping the revs down, doing all the right things, and twice now the car has broken – once because of a bad batch of universal couplings, and the second time because of a malfunction in a Lucas ignition box."

Tyrrell's entry for Stewart in 1970 was the March 701. Jackie and Chris Amon again shared the front row, this time in equal cars and Jackie on pole with a time six-tenths of a second faster. This translated immediately into a lead which Jackie held through 27 of 80 laps. He ended that lap with a raucous misfire. Stopping at the pits he received a new ignition box, but this didn't help much and he retired on lap 57.

Two weeks before the 1971 race Jackie stuffed his Tyrrell-Ford 003 into the banking at Silverstone's Copse Corner with a stuck throttle in a non-

Championship race; such shenanigans would make Ken Tyrrell increasingly dubious about the merits of competing in anything but a *Grande Epreuve*. Readied in time for Monaco, 003 was placed on pole by Jackie with a stunning 1.1-second margin over Ickx's Ferrari that translated into an uninterrupted romp to victory, with fastest lap collected on the way. In 1996 the winning bid at Brooks' auction for the overalls he wore that day was £22,425.

Nineteen seventy-two was not Stewart's year, at Monaco or elsewhere. Starting from equal eighth on the grid after a wet practice session he was third for much of the race but was edged back to fourth just before the finish by Lotus-mounted Emerson Fittipaldi, World Champion that season.

In 1973 Stewart and a few intimates were aware that this Monaco Grand Prix would be his last. With Tyrrell-Ford 006 he claimed pole, this time by just a fifth of a second ahead of Ronnie Peterson's Lotus. After the initial argy-bargy Jackie was into the lead by the eighth lap and held on to it to the finish. He won by just over a second from Emerson Fittipaldi, who set fastest lap. Any win at Monte Carlo is well-earned. This was especially so.

Jackie Stewart has since returned many times to Monte Carlo, the city that more than any other symbolises Grand Prix racing. "I look forward to Monte Carlo every spring," he said. "It would be strange not to. Apart from being a very challenging race track, it has a unique charm. When you get out of the aircraft at Nice and drive along the Riviera to Cap Ferrat and Beaulieu and Monaco in the sunshine, past all those beautiful places, it is very exciting.

"You drive up the hill which is really the circuit, park your car in front of the Hotel de Paris and are greeted like royalty by the staff, as though you had been a constant visitor there for years. It is a complete little place where everyone who is in town for the Grand Prix stays within easy reach of one another. If they are not in the Hermitage or the Paris, they are probably in the Metropole or on a yacht in the harbour, or nearly within walking distance. You hardly need to use a car; you can even walk to the pits."

Jackie Stewart was still walking to the pits in the late 1990s. His affection for the track and race at Monte Carlo was reciprocated. In 1997 the Monaco race gave his and his son Paul's new Formula 1 team, Stewart Grand Prix, a podium position: Rubens Barrichello in the Ford-powered Stewart SF-1 started tenth on the grid and placed second behind Michael Schumacher on a wet track in only their fifth race.

"I've never been happier in my whole career," said Jackie. "Not from a victory, not from a championship. Never. It meant a tremendous amount to know that my son Paul and I had done this together, and maybe the fact that it was at Monaco put more icing on the cake. It was a very big experience."

John Young Stewart was back in a big way in the sport he once dominated – and the sport, in case you hadn't already guessed, was all the better for that.

The Monegasque Guard has the best view of the finish of the 1973 Grand Prix as Jackie brings Tyrrell-Ford 006/2 over the line to win. Before the 1971 start (overleaf) pole-sitting Stewart ignores Louis Chiron's half-minute warning and checks the Royal Box. In less than two hours he's there again to collect his trophy. Jacky Ickx's Ferrari finishes third.

course
MOTUL
elf
elf
5
Gordon

J. STEWART
Ford
GOODYEAR
FORD
elf
Tyrrell
Autolite
4
11

30 secondes

In 1965 Stewart, then second, is just lapping Mike Hailwood's Lotus-BRM and Jo Bonnier's white-striped Brabham-Climax. Jackie lifts a BRM wheel coming over the crest at Mirabeau on his way to a third-place finish.

Jackie pressurises John Surtees's Ferrari in the early laps of the 1966 race (left) until the Italian car breaks its differential and Stewart collects the victory. In 1969 (right) it is Jackie's turn to have u-joint failures in his Matra-Ford.

Jackie is quick to congratulate team-mate Graham Hill (above) after his 1965 lap of honour. The following year (facing page) it's his turn to collect the silverware from Princess Grace under the gaze of Prince Rainier in Jesse Alexander's portrait. The atmosphere is more subdued after Stewart's 1973 victory (below) as the British anthem is played. Pipers would have been more appropriate.

Stewart's second visit to the Monegasque Royal Box (left and centre) is in 1971 when he enjoys a massive advantage over his rivals, shattering the lap record and winning with a 26-second margin over Ronnie Peterson's March-Ford. Young

bespectacled Prince Albert looks on. A burst of sunshine at Monte Carlo during the wet 1972 meeting (right) gives Michael Cooper a fine portrait of Grand Prix racing's golden couple.

Annotated bibliography

Autocourse, 1969–70 (Haymarket Press, 1969). 215pp, hundreds of b/w and colour photographs: 'The Tyrrell Organisation' by David Phipps

A look at the Stewart/Matra/Tyrrell team in its first Championship year as part of the annual *Autocourse* post-season review. Includes a memorable quote from Walter Hayes.

Autoweek, November 1970, 'Jackie Stewart: Variety of Thoughts'

JYS voices his thoughts on sponsors, a second US Grand Prix, safety, Ford and Dunlop's withdrawal from racing. It seems hard to believe that this was 28 years ago.

Ball, Adrian (Ed.), *My Greatest Race by Twenty of the Finest Motor Racing Drivers of All Time* (E. P. Dutton & Co. Inc., 1974). 139pp, 68 b/w photographs

A varied collection of motor-racing aces choose their greatest race. JYS picks the 1968 German GP which he won in truly appalling conditions.

Bentley, John, *The Grand Prix Carpetbaggers (The Autobiography of John Cooper with John Bentley)* (Doubleday & Company Inc, 1977)

An almost-forgotten book these days with foreword by Ken Tyrrell and a brief mention of JYS at the start of his single-seater career. Explains how Stewart extricated himself from an Esso contract so that he could join Tyrrell, who used Shell.

Blunsden, John, 'Jackie Stewart' (*Sports Car Graphic*, September 1966)

An early career overview of JYS, this one post-Spa-shunt, describes Stewart's fiscal shrewdness and his then-family business background. Blunsden compares JYS with Stirling Moss, finding physical and operating similarities.

Brabham, Jack, *When the Flag Drops* (William Kimber, 1971). 240pp, 33 b/w photographs

This is a good read, in fact quite the opposite of what you might have expected from someone as taciturn as JB. Stewart is only featured in the closing part of the book.

Bulgin, Russell, 'Jackie Stewart: Business for Pleasure' (*Motor,* 14 January 1984)

The Stewart *modus operandi* and philosophies as described to journalist Russell Bulgin. What comes across is that JYS is a workaholic. Never still, never too long in any one place, and perhaps never too satisfied or complacent.

Connery, Sean; Davies, Hunter; Dymock, Eric; Gauld, Graham; MacLean, Alistair; McIlvanney, Hugh; Turner, Stuart; Tyrrell, Ken; and Stewart, Jackie *The Exciting World of Jackie Stewart* (William Collins Sons & Co. Ltd, 1974). 88pp

Despite the naff title and multitude of authors this is better than it sounds. Plenty of photographs let down by 1970s layout and poor printing but the whole gives a reasonable overview of JYS and his lifestyle despite its truncated format. It includes a chapter on why Stewart retired, revealing yet again how shrewd and forward-thinking he is.

Crombac, Gerard, *Cars in Profile. No 10 Matra MS 80* (1969/1970). 24pp, 37 b/w photographs, 2 cutaway drawings, 6 colour illustrations

One of the excellent Profile series from the second run which are wonderful sources of potted information. This one features the 1969 Matra F1 car which took JYS to his first World Championship.

Cutter, Robert and Fendell, Bob, *The Encyclopedia of Auto Racing Greats* (Prentice-Hall Inc. 1973). 675pp, hundreds of b/w photographs

Large book trying to cover even larger subject. JYS has 4 1/2 pages which does not quite include his third World Championship, having been written mid-season 1973.

Donaldson, Gerald, *Grand Prix People (Revelations from Inside the F1 Circus)* (MRP Ltd, 1990). 352pp, 29 colour photographs, 78 b/w photographs

Canadian author Donaldson is better known for his biographies of G. Villeneuve and J. Hunt. This is all about the insiders in F1 (drivers, managers, engineers, designers, mechanics, journalists and pundits) and their opinions on the 'circus'. JYS rates 3 pages which is more than some, but it is surprising and depressing how many have moved on or gone since this was written.

Dymock, Eric, 'Jackie Stewart. The Person behind the Driver Analysed' (*Motor,* 13 December 1969)

Essentially a taster for Dymock's book *Jackie Stewart. World Champion*, written together with Stewart, which followed early in 1970. Interestingly the question of the liking or disliking of JYS crops up, which encapsulates the effect Stewart had on the racing fans of the time. Mention is also made of the Mark McCormack organisation which made him less accessible and more expensive.

Falconer, Richard and Nye, Doug, *Chaparral* (Motorbooks International, 1992). 208pp, hundreds of b/w photographs, 29 colour photographs

Superb book on the most successful and most innovative of all American sports-racing cars. Stewart drove the infamous 2J 'sucker' car and Jim Hall was impressed.

Ferrari, Enzo, *Piloti, Che Gente ...* (Conti Editore Bologna, 1985). 479pp, hundreds of photographs

Large-format book with more pictures than text, fascinating and a must for prancing horse aficionados. This English-language edition has some quaint translations and features an autographed picture of JYS driving a 330 P4 at the BOAC 500 at Brands Hatch in 1967. Plus 125 words on him by Enzo.

Fittipaldi, Emerson and Hayward, Elizabeth, *Flying on the Ground* (William Kimber, 1973). 256pp, 29 b/w photographs

One of the last of the Kimber racing books, formulaic in style but good length and well written. Chapter XIII starts 'There is no doubt in my mind that at the moment Jackie Stewart is the best driver in the world.' This really says it all from one of Stewart's chief rivals of the period. As an aside, look at the last photograph in the book and compare to latter-day F1 racing (sic).

Gardner, Derek, 'You Must Win' (*Motor,* 23 October 1971)

The title is ascribed to Ken Tyrrell, and Derek Gardner was of course the Tyrrell designer who went on to create the P34 6-wheeler. He describes how he designed the first Tyrrell even though his racing experience was limited solely to transmission layouts and four-wheel-drive installations (Hobbs Transmissions, Harry Ferguson Research). Just how belt-and-braces his initial approach was can hardly be appreciated in this high tech age. A very interesting article indeed.

Gauld, Graham, *Ecurie Ecosse. A Social History of Motor Racing from the Fifties to the Nineties* (Graham Gauld Public Relations Ltd, 1992). 210pp, many b/w photographs

One man's homage to a team and a way of life long since passed. Stewart's involvement came at a vital point in his career during 1963 and 1964, when he won races in both the Cooper Monaco and two of the Tojeiro coupés. Stewart writes fondly of team patron David Murray, and of course his elder brother had driven for the team in the early 50s. Of particular interest is the signed contract (sic) reproduced on p91 for the 1964 season offering a minimum retaining fee of £500 payable in instalments of £50! No JYS signature ever came cheaper.

Gauld, Graham, 'Jackie Stewart' (*Road & Track*, January 1965)

Abbreviated biography actually written before October 1964 which concerns itself with Stewart's forthcoming F1 career. As with Moss before him, Gauld notes that 'many people in England think he is getting there too soon and too easily.' The doubters were wholly wrong.

Gill, Barrie; Frewin, Leslie, *The Men* (London, 1968). 224pp, 55 photographs

A collection of essays on drivers all racing in 1968 including

JYS. Written before he became World Champion for the first time, good on detail and some long-forgotten anecdotes.

Hayward, Elizabeth, 'Who is A.N. Other? Jackie Stewart, World Champion, That's Who!' (*Road & Track*, January 1970). 5pp

A full-length article on JYS, his racing provenance, family, lifestyle and early Swiss residence. His ultra-busy life is commented on and the 'A.N. Other' of the title refers to his deliberate anonymity at the beginning of his racing career.

Hayward, Elizabeth, 'Jackie Stewart' (*Road & Track*, April 1971)

A brief resumé of JYS, his career and his attitudes which is entirely uncritical, in fact eulogistic. Probably written in late 1970 before the next season started, it was surely a filler article.

Heglar, Mary Schnall, *The Grand Prix Champions* (Bond Parkhurst Books, 1973). 234pp, 102 b/w photographs

Comprised of brief biographies of 14 drivers starting with Nino Farina, ending with Emerson Fittipaldi and including JYS. It was written before his final season and covers largely familiar ground with some emphasis on the tragedies of 1970. It also contains a shocking footnote which tells how JYS was not informed of his father's death whilst at the Argentine GP (which he won) until after the race. Another example of how things have changed.

Henry, Alan (Ed.), *John Surtees, World Champion* (Hazelton Publishing, 1991). 240pp, 98 b/w photographs, 24 colour photographs

Given the man's trenchant views and tendency to be plain speaking this book reads as if it is pulling its punches. Nevertheless well worth reading especially if you are a 1950s–60s bike fan. JYS gets a brief mention for beating Surtees at Silverstone in May 1965, a result ascribed to Ferrari's lack of testing.

Hill, Graham, *Life at the Limit* (William Kimber, 1969). 255pp, 34 b/w photographs

Motor racing old-style and for those under 30 it may come as a surprise to discover that F1 was not always dominant. Hill was typical of this genre, driving nearly everything and anything that came his way. JYS of course represented the first of the new generation of specialists who took over F1, and Hill's time with JYS at BRM saw the Scot benefit enormously from this relationship. Occasionally funny but inevitably superficial as was the custom of the time.

Hunston, Hugh, 'President of Menial Tasks'. (*Pell Mell & Woodcote*, RAC, 1998).

Complimentary view of Stewart Grand Prix and JYS in their first season.

IMPA Bulletin, Vol. 9 No. 6, October 1970

This issue of the International Motor Press Association journal featured JYS answering questions put by Judy Stropus, Pete Lyons, Steve Wilder, Dick Bauer, Wade Hoyt and others about his then-recent Chaparral 2J drive and future plans. Also included were some heavily-critical comments on circuit safety.

Lawrence, Mike, *The Story of March (Four Guys and a Telephone)* (Aston Publications, 1989). 256pp, many b/w and colour photographs

How to launch a racing car company and sell your F1 car for the best driver in the world to drive, on a wing and a prayer. The *modus operandi* of March c1970 is an eye opener for the uninitiated and Mike Lawrence has written a very good book. As for JYS, he managed to win a Grand Prix for March but was never happy with the 701. Tyrrell very quickly produced their own car which appeared later in 1970. No March ever won another Grand Prix.

Manso, Peter, *Vroom!!* (Funk & Wagnalls, 1969), 227pp, 105 photographs

American Peter Manso in one-to-one conversations with ten drivers of the period, some recently retired. In 29 JYS dialogue pages the subjects range from the Spa shunt – which obviously seriously frightened Stewart – to discussing contemporary icons like Frank Sinatra. It ends with the author and Stewart arguing over the US Marines, of all things, and Stewart remarking that not all of their subject material had been relevant. Nevertheless Manso went on to write *Faster!* in conjunction with JYS.

McCall, Chris, 'Hey, Jackie Stewart!' US Grand Prix Report, *Car and Driver*, December 1965

Personalised version of the 1965 Watkins Glen Grand Prix which includes some background on JYS and his image. Miss McCall's insightful writing is in stark contrast to the 'It was lap 12 and he retired' style which typified most British journals of the time.

Nye, Doug, *The Grand Prix Tyrrells. The Jackie Stewart Cars 1970–1973* (Macmillan London Ltd, 1975), 80pp, 100 b/w photographs, 10 colour photographs

Early Nye work with brief Tyrrell background up to 1969 and thereafter the story of the Tyrrell race cars in which Stewart won two World Championships. This is one of a series of similar books based on the Donington collection and although relatively short is very well informed and nicely complemented by the photographs. Poignant too, when one considers how successful Tyrrell was and what became of the team in latter years.

Nye, Doug, *Cooper Cars* (Osprey, 1983). 376pp, hundreds of photographs

The definitive Cooper book which reminds us that JYS also drove a Formula 2 Cooper-BRM T75 occasionally for Ken Tyrrell in 1965, which alas was not a success.

Orr, Frank, (*Track & Traffic*, November 1969)

Column in a Canadian magazine discussing sports popularity in the media and with the general public. At this time motor racing and JYS were becoming world attractions and Stewart, his racing and his pro-active role in safety are discussed. Another example of just how influential Stewart became.

Pritchard, Anthony, *The World Champions, Guiseppe Farina to Jackie Stewart* (Macmillan Publishing Co. Inc, 1974) 253pp, 41 b/w photographs

A series of potted biographies which cover the World Champion drivers from the first, Farina to JYS in 1973 who gets 23 pages. Nothing new here, but a Stewart source nevertheless.

Roebuck, Nigel, *Grand Prix Greats (A Personal Appreciation of 25 Famous Formula 1 Drivers)* (Patrick Stephens Ltd, 1986). 216pp, 149 photographs & 25 portrait paintings

The author's personal choice of F1 aces, and who better to judge. JYS sits well in this company. Once again his analytical and wholly-committed approach to everything (not just racing) shines through.

Rudd, Tony, *It Was Fun! My Fifty Years of High Performance* (Patrick Stephens Ltd, 1993)

This book is so dense with detail that you need to read it again to catch all the things you missed the first time. The BRM saga is particularly interesting given Rudd's central role from V-16 to H-16, both of which flattered only to deceive. In between, however, were the glory years when JYS had his first Grand Prix win in a BRM at Monza in 1965. Be warned however that a knowledge of engines and how they work helps if you want to get the most from this tome. JYS writes the foreword and Rudd, who first saw Stewart dominating the Monaco F3 race in 1964, is a fan.

Scheckter, Jody, *Jody, An Autobiography* (Hugh Keartland Publishers (Pty) Ltd., 1976). 128pp, 75 b/w photographs, 11 colour photographs

Written while Jody was still a Tyrrell driver with foreword by Ken Tyrrell who holds up Stewart as an example to follow. Scheckter in fact benefited from Stewart's advice before and during his tenure at Ockham and of course went on to become World Champion for Ferrari in 1979 (the last Ferrari World Champion!).

Seidler, Edouard, *Champion of the World* (Automobile Year, 1970). 109pp, many colour & b/w photographs

This is really a promotional book for Elf and Matra and their participation in motorsport of the period which of course includes Stewart's 1969 World Championship. Much of the content is concerned with other French drivers and various racing formulae which reminds one of just how determined *la belle France* was to succeed at international motorsport. Photographs are numerous and varied but too many are deliberately blurred, an irritating feature of the period.

Small, Steve, *The Grand Prix Who's Who* (Guinness Publishing Ltd, 1996, 2nd edition). 464pp, hundreds of b/w photographs

A detailed reference work on every Grand Prix driver and the cars they drove from 1950 to date of publication, very useful and helpful as a cross-check on the events described in the book. Stewart is on page 400.

Stanley, Louis, *Grand Prix. The Legendary Years – The Personal Memoirs of Louis Stanley* (Queen Anne Press, 1994). 248pp, hundreds of b/w photographs

An interesting and sometimes controversial book from the unique Louis Stanley. His opinions on JYS and the Scot's frantic lifestyle are surely spot-on.

Stewart, Jackie, 'On Your Jack' (*Autocar*, 27 May 1966)

This article by JYS is ostensibly about Jack Brabham but it actually includes comments on the forthcoming season, other competitors and a substantial section on how JYS learns a circuit.

Stewart, Jackie, *Car's Competition News*, February 1969

Yet another version of Stewart's career to date albeit by JYS himself in *Car's* racing supplement plus comments on entrant John Coombs.

Stewart, Jackie, *Car's Competition News*, June 1969

As above, a column penned by JYS for *Car Magazine*'s motorsports supplement of the time. Blunt words on safety, specifically after the Spanish GP crashes, and details of his recent races plus thoughts on various and associated activities.

Stewart, Jackie with Dymock, Eric, *Jackie Stewart: World Champion* (Henry Regnery Company, 1970). 192pp, 29 b/w photographs

A book written in conjunction with a journalist, fellow Scot Eric Dymock. It features a brief biography up to 1964 and thereafter concerns itself mainly with Stewart's F1 career, culminating in his first World Championship (1969). The text is divided into two parts, Dymock's comments appearing in italics, and is written in chronological order. As in *Faster!* there are comments on fellow drivers and personalities but rather less critical. This is a good if somewhat abbreviated account covering a fairly limited period, obviously capitalising on Stewart's 1969 World Championship.

Stewart, Jackie and Manso, Peter, *Faster! A Racer's Diary* (Farrar, Straus and Giroux, 1972). 239pp, 11 b/w photographs.

This diarised book covers a year in the life of JYS (1970) and at times is necessarily reflective, almost melancholic as McLaren, Courage and Rindt all perished in this tragic season. It provides a realistic insight not only into Stewart's *raison d'être* but also into the risks involved nearly 30 years ago. The safety concerns over Spa are stated very strongly indeed and illustrate perfectly the polarisation Stewart caused in motorsports. His opinions on some of his fellow competitors are less than complimentary but time and tide have proved him right. Fascinatingly and ironically it reads better today than it did when first published, perhaps because we can all now appreciate fully his contribution to survival in motor racing.

Taylor, Simon; Henry, Alan; Goodwin, Colin; Cropley, Steve with Stewart, Jackie, 'Stewart Ford. The inside story of a new Grand Prix team's race to the Formula 1 grid' (*Autocar*, 1997). 34pp

Promotional magazine describing the launching of the Stewart GP team in 1997 which at the time of writing has a distinctly over-optimistic tone.

Time, 1 August 1969

Two and a bit columns describing JYS, his background, his relationship with Jim Clark and what is described as 'cautious conservatism'. His description of a car being 'really very much like a woman' adding 'one day you have to be gentle, the next you may have to give it a good thrashing' would never be published today, especially not in America.

Tremayne, David, 'The Best Driver in the World' (*Autosport*, 18/25 December 1997)

The title is courtesy of Ken Tyrrell and this excellent piece by David Tremayne captures the essence of JYS and his ability to make the right decisions nearly every time. Few realise the extraordinary work load he put himself through in 1970–72 and his resultant health problems, but of course he bounced back.

Turner, Philip, 'Into the Big Time. The Noviciate of John Young Stewart' (*Motor*, 11 December 1965)

JYS certainly attracted media attention and here is yet another praising piece by *Motor*'s well-liked Sports Editor which looks back at his 1965 season and forward to the new 3-litre F1 formula, which I seem to remember was hyped as 'The Return of Power'.

Webb, Ben, 'Life in This Very Fast Lane' (*Enterprise*, January/February 1997)

Article on the formation of the Stewart Grand Prix Team before its launch in 1997.

Yamaguchi, Jack, 'Fuji 200' (*Road & Track*, January 1967)

Did you know that an Indy-style race was run on the Fuji International Speedway in Japan in late 1966? It had a very complete entry with JYS, Graham Hill, Chris Amon, Jim Clark, Mario Andretti, Bobby Unser and other Indy regulars. Practice problems with oil starvation saw 10 N/S including Clark, whilst Hill and Stewart along with Canadian Billy Foster shared the lead. Eventually Foster and Hill retired leaving JYS to win from Bobby Unser.

Young, Eoin, 'Championship Year?' (*Autocar*, 1 April 1966)

Overly-optimistic title for JYS after his successful inaugural F1 season with BRM in 1965. Written when Young was a contemporary reporter it mentions the Monza win and Stewart's thoughts on the forthcoming 3-litre formula. Unfortunately he was going to drive the H-16 BRM, and it was just as well that BRM had the old V-8 cars in 2-litre Tasman form to fall back on.

Young, Eoin, 'Jackie Stewart' (*Road & Track*, April 1966)

Not surprisingly much the same content as the *Autocar* article, with a typically close-up colour pic by Jesse Alexander at Spa 1965 to illustrate the text.

Young, Eoin, 'Jackie Stewart. The Total Racing Driver' (*Autocar*, 25 October 1973)

Written soon after Stewart's retirement and the tragic death of François Cévert, this is a précis of the JYS career. On reflection it seems odd that Young, along with other contemporary journos who wrote so many articles on JYS, did not produce a definitive racing biography.

Photograph credits

Jesse Alexander: P72, P96, P197.

Bernard Cahier: P10, P46 upper, P47 upper, P48, P65 upper, P80–81, P83 lower, P85, P111, P114, P122 upper & lower, P123 upper & lower, P126 lower, P133 upper, P140, P151 upper, P155 lower left & right, P157 lower right, P158, P173, P174 upper & lower, P175 upper right & lower left & right, P178–179 upper & lower, P181 upper, P196 upper, P198 left.

Michael Cooper: P17 upper left & upper right, P20–21, P41 lower, P60 upper & lower, P64 lower, P79, P84 upper & lower, P86–87, P88 upper & lower, P89 upper & lower, P121, P124–125, P132 lower, P134, P135 upper & lower, P151 middle & lower, P152 upper left & right, P153 lower left & right, P154 upper right & lower left, P157 lower left, P167, P170–171, P172 lower, P180 lower, P181 lower, P184, P199 right.

Eric della Faille from Alexis Callier Collection: P17 lower, P150 left, P180 upper, P191, P196 lower.

Graham Gauld: P22, P29, P30, P31 upper left & upper right & lower, P33, P34, P35 upper, middle, lower, P36 upper & lower, P37, P56 left & right, P57 upper & lower, P64 upper left & right, P147, P148 upper, middle & lower, P149 left & right, P150 right, P156 upper left & lower.

Indianapolis Motor Speedway: P66–67.

Trevor Legate: P169 lower, P176–177.

Max Le Grand: Frontispiece, P155 upper left.

Max Le Grand from Ludvigsen Library: P40 upper & lower, P41 upper, P55, P58–59, P61, P82 lower, P90–91, P92 upper & lower, P93 lower, P97, P98 upper, P99, P100 upper & lower left, P100 upper right, P101 left & right, P102 upper & lower, P104–105, P106 left & right, P107, P108–109, P110, P128, P152 lower left, P155 upper right, P157 upper, P165, P192–193, P194 left & right, P195 left & right, P198–199 middle.

Karl Ludvigsen from Ludvigsen Library: P18–19, P42-43, P44 upper, P44-45 lower, P45 upper, P46 lower, P100 lower right, P127 upper, P129 lower, P138 upper, middle & lower, P139, P156 upper right, P166 upper, middle & right, P168 left & right, P169 upper, P172 upper.

Ludvigsen Library: P38–39 upper, P47 lower, P113, P126 upper, P127 lower, P129 upper & middle, P130–131, P132 upper, P133 lower, P136–137, P153 upper left & right, P175 upper left.

Ove Nielssen from Ludvigsen Library: P182–183.

Stanley Rosenthall from Ludvigsen Library: P38–39 lower, P65 lower, P68 upper & lower, P82 upper, P83 upper, P93 upper, P94–95, P98 lower, P103, P154 upper left & lower right.

H. P. Seufert: P152 lower right.

Nigel Snowdon: P112.

Jack Yamaguchi: P69 upper & lower, P70–71.

Index

CARS INDEX

FER